Midnight's Grandchildren

T0384156

While the west has experienced multiple post-war economic, social and political revolutions, India by contrast has had two distinct moments of transformation in the past century: Independence in 1947 and the economic liberalisation that began in 1991. Midnight's Grandchildren are the off-spring of India's second social and economic revolution.

India's millennial generation, coming of age post-1991, have grown up in a world of opportunity and relative abundance. Many institutions – family, marriage, workplace, and brands – are being disrupted. Great tension exists as a new generation breaks barriers and seeks to find its place. This book captures an important, transformative moment in India's development. It includes interviews with young Indians who articulate both their optimism and the struggle to find relevant new identities. Managers and recruiters speak about the changes in the workplace and the challenges and opportunities of harnessing India's so-called demographic dividend. Entrepreneurs, brand owners and marketers discuss the role of brands in cementing identities in a world changing rapidly where loyalty has little meaning.

Midnight's Grandchildren explains for a business audience the significance of the arrival in the workforce of a generation of millennials as both disruptors of the old order and engine of India's future economic potential. It is of use for professionals and educators wanting to engage this vitally important group of young people.

Mark Hannant is a creative services entrepreneur. He has extensive experience of working in the places where emerging and developed markets meet, and is the co-founder and managing director of magenta, a fresh-thinking creative agency based in Mumbai. He has appeared in two Bollywood movies.

Midnight's Grandchildren

How Young Indians Are Disrupting
the World's Largest Democracy

Mark Hannant

Routledge
Taylor & Francis Group

LONDON AND NEW YORK

First published 2019
by Routledge
2 Park Square, Milton Park, Abingdon, Oxon OX14 4RN

and by Routledge
605 Third Avenue, New York, NY 10017

First issued in paperback 2021

Routledge is an imprint of the Taylor & Francis Group, an informa business

British Library Cataloguing-in-Publication Data
A catalogue record for this book is available from the British Library

Library of Congress Cataloging-in-Publication Data
Names: Hannant, Mark, author.
Title: Midnight's grandchildren : how young Indians are disrupting the
world's largest democracy / Mark Hannant.
Description: Abingdon, Oxon ; New York, NY : Routledge, 2019. |
Includes bibliographical references and index. |
Identifiers: LCCN 2018035631 (print) |
LCCN 2018037758 (ebook) | ISBN 9780429456701 (ebook) |
ISBN 9781138314832 (hardback : alk. paper)
Subjects: LCSH: Economic development–India–History–21st century. |
Generation Y–India. | Demographic transition–India. |
Organizational change–India. | Social change–India. | India–Economic
conditions–21st century. | India–Social conditions–21st century.
Classification: LCC HC435.3 (ebook) |
LCC HC435.3 .H354 2019 (print) | DDC 338.954–dc23
LC record available at https://lccn.loc.gov/2018035631

ISBN 13: 978-0-367-78762-2 (pbk)
ISBN 13: 978-1-138-31483-2 (hbk)

Typeset in Sabon
by Swales & Willis Ltd, Exeter, Devon, UK

For my grandfather John Hannant, whose adventurous spirit inspired me to see the world.

Contents

Acknowledgements

Thanks first to Jonathan Norman who saw the potential for a book and suggested it after our 'Groucho Breakfast' in London in May 2016 and to John Smythe for the invitation to speak at that event. I'm grateful to Kristina Abbots for picking up the project at Routledge when Jonathan moved on and extending a patient and helping hand to a first-time author.

My gratitude to James Gill and Paul Laurence who advised me on the commercial and legal points of contract negotiations. Drinks on me!

Immense appreciation is due to each of my interview subjects who gave generously of their time and, without whom, there wouldn't be a book.

Thank you: Bimal Bhatt, Rakshit Patel and 'Jay', Pawan Jani, Amrit Thomas, PK Padmakumar, R Nanda, Heather Saville Gupta, Omkar, and the gang at Austere including Nalini Indiran, Nivaskar Perumal, Kartick Moorthi, Keerthi Selvan, Kartick Thirumalai, Sweta Sinha, and Tarun Sinha; at Rickshaw, Bidisha Roy, Manveen Ahuja, Sanjana Kothari, and Stacy Samuel; Shantanu Raj, Shiraz Mukherjee, and Kanchi Pandya; Naresh Fernandes; Sunil Sood, and Sandeep Batra at Vodafone, Julia Manke, Kalpana Medbalmi, Amruda Nair, Kanika Tekriwal; Kartikeya Tutwala and Prashant Dagwar; Nikunj Shah, Subrata Dey, Bernadine Swamy, Raj Aditya Chaudhuri, Surekha Rao, Viren Arora, and Abhiram Eleswarapu. I'm grateful to Sujaya Banerjee for the early conversation that set the seed of the idea in place.

Thanks to Sunanda Parekh for being a frequent advocate and for introducing Kanika Subbiah. Ruby Thapar offered encouragement and useful perspective along the way.

Niraj Pamwani was a perennial source of entertainment and guided me through the intricacies of life in Bollywood and the underbelly of Bombay and made sure I got home in one piece. धन्यवाद, dhanyavaad.

Jonathan Bill was an enthusiastic travelling partner, physically and figuratively, and a super sounding board, willing to talk though ideas and experiences and help me decode the complexities of India and its business culture. Cheers, man! Thanks to Swati Ladd for always having an encouraging word to share. Shoba Purushotaman and Anthony Hayward shared much of the India adventure with us, provided plentiful hospitality, and gave a broader perspective on the entrepreneurial journey. Mahua Hazarika contributed a lot and has been a invaluable source of ideas and perspective throughout the process.

Andre Morris and Niloufer Venkatramen have offered steadfast friendship and thoughtful advice over the years and the chance to escape the city once in a while. Niloufer did a sterling job of reading the manuscript and giving valuable pointers as it evolved while Andre had the children away at camp providing the 'head space' needed to finish the text. Thanks, much!

Lucy Unger has been a great mate, generous host, and cherished professional confidant for much of my time in India. She provided insightful review of the original outline and made several important introductions. Many thanks.

Thank you to our talented and hard-working teams at magenta and Indigo Premedia (millennials all but two!) who compensated for my absence from the office and the lack of attention to project work when I was there: Altaf Ansari, Nupur Tutwala, Anusha Singh, Dhanya Menon, Ritika Arya, Arun Sankar, Jaideep Dave, Vini Avlani, Shivani Patel, Soumik Roy, Sweta Gajjar, Apurva Kadam, Needhi Bharmani, and

Kinnari Gala. Salomi Shah, our info graphics queen, did a really great job to interpret my words and develop a lovely illustration style to liven up the pages. A big thanks to our clients, whose continued faith and support pays the bills every month.

I found that distance running helped to manage the effort required to complete the work. As I came to realise, a book requires stamina. There's no external momentum. You have to put in the hard miles. There are no short cuts though competent and enthusiastic assistance can reduce the burden somewhat. Thanks to Alan Rosling for some practical tips as I embarked on the process.

Thanks to the attentive team at Manoribel, my writing den an hour-and-a-half, and a world away, from central Mumbai. The thrill of watching as horses and traps thundered along the beach remains vivid. The sadness as I witnessed a baby's corpse washed up and buried on the beach haunts me. I was forced to confront the terrible reality of the odds stacked against females in India from the moment of conception and throughout their lives. Her mother, I surmise, was a millennial for whom freedom and independence are yet a distant dream, who experiences a female child as an unwanted encumbrance.

I owe thanks to the many people in Mumbai and further afield who have welcomed me, and Munni, into their lives in the past decade. Special thanks to Jyotsna Changrani and Siddharth Rastogi, Ravi and Els Kini, Nikunj and Seema Shah, Shantanu and Lata Sarkara. In Bhavanagar, Munni's aunt and uncle Rama and Sharad Oza and her cousins Devu, Alka and Chintan have made us welcome and ensured we retained links to a 'native place'. Thank you all. In Singapore, Kiran Kandade allowed us free rein of her apartment as we set up Indigo Premedia. We love you for that and your unstinting friendship. Friends back in London have been fervent supporters and liberal in their hospitality whenever we've been back in the Smoke. Big thanks to Sam and Dan Cane, Annie Stork and Matthew Bench, Jo and Tim Sennitt, Hans and Anne Towler, Paul Richmond and Fiona McLeod. Gurinder and Rita Atwal have been tremendous at both a practical and emotional level over the years. We owe you much. I will come and clear our stuff from the loft! In Brighton 'Uncle Plug' and 'Mrs Fish' have been generous throughout the adventure. You're with us in spirit even though sadly we've failed to entice you to experience the mayhem first hand.

My father David and late mother Rosemary bequeathed me a moral compass that has sustained me. I saw in them, and then instituted for myself, a work ethic that has permitted me the freedom and confidence to make non-conformist life choices and allowed me to make the most of my limited talents. Your love and advice are greatly appreciated. Thank you too to the wonderful Helen who has made my father's later years such a rich period and who has been an inspirational, rather youthful, 'grandma' to our children. Thank you to my siblings Shona and Erica for your love and support and interest throughout.

Munni has been a partner and confidant throughout the past 20 years. Thank you for your love and friendship and for giving me the courage to embark on this. Thanks for taking up the slack at home and in the office while I spent time writing, and for helping me manage the mental and emotional skirmishes that came with it. I know it's taken a toll and I am forever indebted. Without you none of this would exist. Team!

Our beautiful and inspirational offspring, Milan John and Maya Rose, have put up with my absences and distraction during the process. 'You do seem to have been a bit stressed, Daddy', observed one! Thank you for taking care of Mummy when I wasn't there. Whether as your lives unfold, you stay in India or find adventure, happiness, and meaning elsewhere, it will always be a part of you; and you a part of it.

Mumbai
October 2018

Introduction

This book is the product of a love affair. Not with India but with an Indian. She was first a colleague, later girlfriend, then fiancée, and since the millennium, my wife. She is Munni. Professionally she's a partner in two businesses that we've built together over the past decade. She's the mother to our two children. Ethnically half Indian, they were born into the melting pot of early 21st-century gentrification in the Borough of Hackney in London's East End.

On our first date in a dimly lit, now defunct, bar on Islington's Essex Road, more than 20 years ago, we'd spoken about India. She's a migrant twice over. Born in Uganda, to parents who'd migrated from India in the years after Independence, she'd moved to the UK as a six-year-old, her father presciently fearful of the changes threatened by the arrival in power of Idi Amin following a military coup the year before. She grew up in an industrial town on the banks of the Manchester Ship Canal, enjoyed school and college, where she excelled, and then moved to London to work. Over one too many rum and Cokes (no good ever comes of it), she told me about the year she'd spent in India after college, getting to know her cousins, to whom she was something of an exotic alien, and learning to speak Gujarati, her mother's native tongue but one she'd never learnt at home.

I asked if she ever planned to live in India? 'Maybe', she said.

India was in my peripheral vision since my earliest memories but despite having travelled in South East Asia, I had never been to the subcontinent.

My maternal aunt had departed on a ship from Southampton to Bombay a year before my birth. During the next 20 years she'd taught at schools in Bombay (now Mumbai), Madras (now Chennai) and Chandigarh. Returning every five years to England, she had been a colourful, and to my mind intrepid visitor, who came bearing gifts of brightly coloured material, woodcarvings, and cassette tapes of traditional Indian folk music. My impression of India was distant, poor, and nebulous.

Munni and I travelled together to India in 1997 and then returned three years later. Accompanied by a gang of friends and family we had a short Hindu wedding ceremony in the shade of pungent neem trees in the quiet garden of her uncle's home in the, even then, gridlocked city of Ahmedabad.

In that sprawling metropolis, Gujarat's commercial and administrative hub, and later in the cities of Bhavnagar, Vadodara, and the megalopolis of Mumbai, I was introduced to a gaggle of nephews and nieces. They were then young children whose names I couldn't pronounce, one or two on the cusp of adolescence, all part of a large extended family to whom I am related primarily through my late mother-in-law's side of the equation. I say primarily because, as is the nature of traditional Indian families, where historically marriage outside a small sub-caste was frowned upon and arranged marriages the norm, she is in some cases related to the same people also through her father's side. A hand-drawn family tree was a helpful addition to the notebook kept at all times in my satchel or by my side. I was an oddity to them but warmly welcomed and treated as the *jamai raj* (son-in-law prince), a place of high esteem in the pecking order and a role I had no difficulty adjusting to!

Other visits to India followed. I could measure the rising prosperity of my cousins-in-law and their contemporaries by the cars they had upgraded to since the last visit, and the steady accumulation of gold jewellery and bigger apartments. And extra inches around their waists. Bankers, engineers, traders, businessmen and -women, and occasional teachers (delighted to know that my parents had spent their professional lives stood at the front of classrooms), they gave generous and warm hospitality. My female cousins-in-law took delight in feeding me. When I said I'd already eaten at another's house the reply was to assure me that the other's food was not to be trusted. Even if she was her sister!

I found the bustle and energy of Mumbai exhilarating. I remember being stuck in a traffic jam in the early hours of a morning on the way to the crumbling old international airport. A Tata Indica, at the time a popular choice with India's upwardly mobile (if not always forwardly mobile) urban professionals, made its spluttering, fume-emitting slow progress past pavements crowded with families busy with their night-time basket weaving. In lean-to shanties nearby, their kinsfolk were ironing clothes, repairing bicycles, cutting hair, and performing a host of other small-scale but vital entrepreneurial activities.

The sights, flavours, and smells of India are intoxicating. Its energy and spirit of enterprise are potent, heady, and exciting too.

I was also drawn on those vacations to the beach bars, spicy seafood, and jaffa sunsets of Goa and to the placid daydream backwaters of Kerala. But as a city-lover it was the Mumbai hustle, its metropolitan diversity, and star-maker vitality that really excited me.

In search of adventure

In early 2009 Munni and I, and two pre-school children, left the calm certainty of leafy north London and moved to Mumbai. We wanted an adventure. We believed the children would benefit from a dose of Indian education. 'They spare no pains, nor yet the rod! To see our tasks done well', proclaims the school song of Bombay Scottish School, Mahim, an institute founded in 1847 by Scottish Presbyterians. Whereas in the days of the Raj Englishmen would send their offspring back 'home' to be educated, we have chosen to do the reverse. We felt our children should learn Indian languages and have a chance to know their Indian-born cousins. And if this is the Asian Century, and India and China will power economic growth over the span of their working lifetimes, we should, we thought, allow them the chance to know this side of their biological heritage and encourage them to flourish in the east.

Some of these things have been achieved. After eating dinner at a famed street-food restaurant on a cool November evening, we walked the mile or so home. My just-about-to-be-ten-year-old daughter stopped at a roadside fruit cart piled high with ripe, sweet smelling guavas and managed the whole process of buying, instructing which were to be given a dab of tangy masala, and paying in Hindi. 'We'd have paid double if you'd opened your mouth and spoken English', she told me with relish as we munched our fruit dessert and dodged the bicycles, auto rickshaws, and 4×4s on the narrow lane home. Whatever else has been accomplished in our time in India, the acquisition of Indian languages by my children is one box ticked. And I gather from reliable sources this includes my daughter's ability to curse fluently in Hindi!

Aside from a loose familial connection there were other motivations. We saw business opportunities that excited.

A decade ago as the so-called sub-prime banking crisis, then global economic crisis, engulfed the British economy and austerity loomed, a fast-growing, rapidly transforming economy in a nation preparing to take its place on the world stage had great appeal.

My professional interest was initially piqued by large-scale acquisitions such as the 2007 deal in which Tata Steel used a combination of low interest rates and high leverage to buy Corus, the Anglo-Dutch conglomerate previously known as British Steel. Corus was at the time a client and as a professional communicator my view was that much that happened in that deal, from a communications perspective, could have been handled better. In retrospect I realised that what was on show was a cultural gulf in which the acquired company expected to be on the receiving end of a major shake-up, a 100-day program in which name plates were swapped and management found themselves on the lookout for new jobs. The acquirers were in fact taking a long-term view and looking to keep the asset running without major disruption but failed to articulate a clear message and vision of where the European business fitted into its long-term plans. 'These guys could do with some better communications support', I thought, and went back to my day job, which at the time also involved using cheap money and unsustainable leverage to buy other marketing communications businesses.

Figure I.1

The Corus deal was followed a year later by the audacious US$2.3 billion purchase orchestrated by then chairman of Tata Sons, Ratan Tata, of Jaguar Land Rover (JLR) by another part of the sprawling Tata conglomerate (Figure I.1). My co-directors and colleagues were incredulous. The world had gone mad they said. How could it be that Indian companies were buying stalwarts of the London Stock Exchange and iconic British brands? (Albeit in the case of JLR ones that had been owned in the interim by other non-British companies.) Hadn't the British, after all, owned India for a couple of hundred years?

My reading of the situation, in part due to a growing familiarity and interest in India, was that the world was changing fundamentally and economic power was shifting east. Investment bankers wrote reports on BRICS (Brazil, Russia, India, China, South Africa) economies. Commentary appeared on the finance pages of the mainstream press about funds diverted to emerging markets with growth rates in double digits. These, and the potential of an emerging middle class in a continent that was home to more than half the world's people, all suggested to me that I should be looking east and placing a professional bet on India. An idea took root that in a market experiencing a major transformation there was potential demand for high-quality communications support. The plan was to build on knowledge of 'what good looks like globally' – to apply the principles by which leading international companies engage their stakeholders – and create a service offering tailored to an Indian context. The vision was to build a creative business that served the needs of companies operating at the intersection of developed and emerging markets. We would be bridge-builders, helping companies and brands speak effectively to new stakeholders.

So, for almost a decade I've been based in Mumbai and had a ringside seat as my nieces and nephews have grown and achieved adulthood in a country that has transformed in many ways during their lives and in the time I've been an India migrant. I have had privileged access into the impeccably manicured boardrooms of major Indian enterprises, with their liveried peons and colonial-era rules of etiquette. I've seen the spectrum of business leaders; some erudite and razor sharp, sometimes impressively understated, others full of hubris, prone to tantrums, or simply out of their depth. Cocooned, and surrounded by deference and 'yes' men, few hear much that is critical.

My colleagues and I at magenta, the branding and communications agency Munni and I founded, have contributed in small ways to some big Indian success stories. Escaping the chill of air-conditioned offices whenever the chance presents itself, I've stepped out across fields and around factories, and sat in offices and canteens, to feel the pulse of a host of businesses from tech giants and fertiliser makers, minerals extractors and chemicals manufacturers to banking start-ups and healthcare innovators.

Living and doing business in India has been simultaneously the greatest challenge and most enriching experience of my five decades on the planet.

The germ of the idea that underpins this book appeared early in my tenure in India. I was sat in a wood-panelled cabin on the 13th floor of Essar House, the headquarters of an ambitious, sometimes controversial, Indian conglomerate with interests in ports, oil and gas, shipping, and, at the time, telecoms via a stake in Vodafone. Its towering headquarters, equipped with a rooftop helipad, overlooks the expanse of South Mumbai's Mahalaxmi Racecourse. Essar's then head of Learning and Development Sujaya Banerjee and I were chatting. We'd been engaged to provide consultancy support to the Essar Oil team, headed by former BP executive Ifty Nasir, who was leading a team that was buying the Stanlow oil refinery in Cheshire, from Shell. The Anglo-Dutch giant had also been a client and I knew its downstream business well from my years in London.

Sujaya was explaining to me how difficult it was to introduce a performance management system in a place where the predominant belief system is Hinduism with its creed of reincarnation and karma. In karmic systems of thought cause and effect are tightly linked to rebirth. What you are today – and importantly where you find yourself in the caste system – is a result of what you did or didn't do in previous lives. Life is preordained. And there are many lives to be led in search of nirvana. In this eternal cycle, what relevance, she asked, are a set of performance measures that changed with the seasons? Traditional Indian culture, manifest in all manner of institutions, including the workplace, is not naturally aligned to quarterly reporting or annual performance reviews.

The discussion also touched on the changes taking place in the workplace as a group of young people, born and raised in a country that is rapidly transforming and for whom life chances are vastly different from those of their parents and grandparents, made their presence felt. Conventional cultural and religious ideas were being jettisoned, she told me. Those shifts go some way to making the introduction of a performance management system more viable, but at the same time they are exposing a host of other fault lines.

As is often the case with significant moments (a date in an Islington bar, for example) their consequence is only revealed and understood much later.

Around seven years later my former colleague John Smythe, founder of Engage for Change and author of the book *Chief Engagement Officer: Turning Hierarchy Upside Down to Drive Performance*, invited us to speak at one of his regular 'Groucho Breakfasts' in London. Munni and I put together a well-received presentation that considered some of the cultural challenges of doing business in India. We drew on Geert Hofstede's work on cultural dimensions and thought about India's 'engagement agenda' at a moment of profound change. We began to organise information and insights on the way in which a generation of young people, India's millennials, were demanding and creating change in the workplace and across many other areas of life. As brand thinkers we're always on the lookout for labels and 'shorthand' descriptors. We coined the term Midnight's Grandchildren to describe them.

Jonathan Norman, who had published John's book, was in the audience and suggested this might make an interesting subject for a book. 'For sure!' I said, confidently, without thinking through the implications. 'Bugger!' I thought, less confidently, when the consequences of time and effort required dawned on me.

What follows is an attempt to describe, draw conclusions, and extract lessons from some of the things I've observed, discussed, and experienced. I see India through multiple lenses: as a business owner, investor, employer, consumer, and parent to two half-Indian children. I wrap those personas into the term 'India migrant' and I use the term deliberately. Evidence supports a belief that migrants, whether internal or transnational, contribute significantly to the economies of their hosts at city, state, or national level. Migrants are entrepreneurial and by definition risk-takers. They create jobs and wealth, not just for themselves but also for other parts of the community. They fill skills gaps and pay taxes. Given the toxicity of the term in contemporary political discourse mine is an attempt to reclaim the word and highlight the fact that economic migrancy comes in many shades.

As a student of sociology and social anthropology 30 years ago I was drawn to the experiential research methodology of 'participant observation' widely used by the likes of Bronislaw Malinowski and Margaret Mead. William Foote Whyte's ethnology of an Italian migrant community in Boston, *Street Corner Society*, left a lasting impression. In my professional activities that desire to uncover and understand at ground level has been honed as a proficiency in 'getting under the skin' of organisations.

For the purpose of this book, participant observation has been my primary model of research. I've interviewed more than 50 people – some millennials by birth, some by attitude, and a host of people who had what I thought were relevant and interesting perspectives to share.

I've tried to balance the sociological, relevant as a frame of reference, the journalistic, a professional modus operandi applied for the past three decades, and the managerial to make it useful for business executives who want real-world tips and takeaways. The aim has been to write a story with character and colour that captures a unique and exciting moment in world history and to provide a manual with practical applications that may provide benefits to anyone who is excited by India and the immense potential it offers now and in coming decades.

Notes on the research

As a time frame for this book I've looked at the changes taking place within a couple of generations. I've considered Midnight's Children to be born in the years after Indian Independence in 1947, to around the mid-1960s. They are elsewhere described as baby boomers and demographers use the period 1946–1964 to frame their arrival. Generation X who came into the world between the mid-1960s and mid-1980s followed them. Millennials, the Indian cohort here described as Midnight's Grandchildren, were born from the mid-1980s to 2000. The next generation, the digitally native Gen Z, as they've been termed, was born in the 21st century.

Interviews were conducted in person between August 2017 and February 2018.

Baby Boomers	Gen 'X'	Millennials	Gen 'Z'
1946-1964	1964-1983	1983-2000	2000-present

Figure I.2

1 Moments of transformation

India has experienced two moments of profound change in the past century.

The nation gained independence in 1947. As 14 August gave way to 15 August almost three centuries of rule, first by the British East India Company and then the British government, came to an end. Turmoil and bloodshed ensued.

For almost a century the Indian independence movement had sought to throw off the shackles of colonial rule. In the movement's latter stages, as the Second World War raged across the globe, some, such as 'Netaji' Subash Chandra Bose, founder of the Indian National Army, sought assistance from Britain's enemies. The All India Congress Committee rallied under the banner of 'Quit India' and supported 'Mahatma' Mohandas Gandhi's strategy of non-violent resistance. In the aftermath of the Second World War, victorious but broke, the British finally recognised that it's ongoing rule of a once prized possession was untenable and began to seriously consider the options for its withdrawal.

The terms of the departure were enshrined in the Indian Independence Act, which included within it partition of the country along religious lines. A Muslim-dominated Pakistan to the north was carved out from the Hindu-majority India and some 15 million people found themselves on the wrong side of the new boundaries. One of the largest migrations in history took place as people either chose or were forced from places that had been their homes for generations. In the ensuing violence between one and two million lives were lost. In a *New Yorker* essay William Dalrymple writes: 'Partition is central to modern identity in the Indian subcontinent, as the Holocaust is to identity among Jews, branded painfully onto the regional consciousness by memories of almost unimaginable violence' (*The New Yorker*, 2015).[1] One of the most destructive enmities in human history was forged as the British beat a hasty and poorly planned retreat. Seventy years later the shadow of partition hangs over a billion and a half lives on a deeply divided subcontinent.

India, which had fought long for its independence but had little time to prepare for it, embarked on a four-decade economic experiment in Nehruvian Socialism. Given its name by the often maligned, recently partially rehabilitated, first prime minister of the newly free nation, Jawaharlal Nehru, this model of command economy was also known as the Licence Raj or Permit Raj. Much influenced by the Soviet Union, with which by the mid-1950s the fledgling Indian state had aligned itself, India had a planning commission that issued five-year plans, and the economy was essentially closed to the rest of the world. Government-owned business prevailed. Inefficiency bred. High tariffs meant foreign-made goods were excluded from the market. Under this system private companies could manufacture only with a government permit. Government controlled who could produce what goods and in what quantities, and at what price they could be sold. The results, as the 1950s and 1960s evolved, were disastrous. The prevailing environment was one of scarcity and lack of opportunity. Monopolies prevailed. Competition was banished. Corruption was rife, not least because of the 'market' in licences that this system instituted. The economy stagnated and for around four decades growth averaged 3–3.5 per cent per annum, disparagingly referred to as the Hindu rate of growth.

In 1991 the Indian government was forced to begin a period of liberalisation when the balance of payments predicament that had been brewing throughout the 1980s worsened and became a full-blown crisis. The government was days away from defaulting on its debt obligations and had to airlift 47 tons of gold to the Bank of England to raise emergency funds. This moment marked the beginning of a period of policy reform, which continues today. The Licence Raj gave way to a more liberal, demand-led form of political economy.

From 1991 the prevailing doctrine shifted towards greater openness, more foreign investment, an emerging, but still not comprehensive, market orientation, and a bigger role for the private sector. Kick-starting the new era of openness when he announced the Union Budget in July 1991, then Finance Minister Manmohan Singh said:

> As Victor Hugo once said, 'no power on Earth can stop an idea whose time has come'. I suggest ... that the emergence of India as a major economic power in the world happens to be one such idea. Let the whole world hear it loud and clear. India is now wide-awake. We shall prevail. We shall overcome.
>
> (Goswami, 2017)[2]

For the past 25 years growth rates have averaged around 6.5 per cent. Corruption has remained endemic.

This bifurcation of 70 years into two precise eras is of course a gross simplification of what has been a hugely complex process of development with twists and turns, false dawns and missed opportunities, hope and expectations. Despite its crudeness I believe it has merit as a frame of reference for the discussion and stories that follow because half of India's population, my nephews and nieces included, was born after 1991. By 2020 it will be the youngest country on the planet with a median age of just

29 years (NDTV, 2017).[3] Its sheer scale – one in six of the world population lives in India – means that what happens in India, economically,
politically, and socially in the coming years, has a bearing on us all.

The Mumbai-born author Salman Rushdie was a few weeks old when
India gained independence. Thirty-four years later he published a book
about that moment in history and the lives of *Midnight's Children*, the
title of his Man Booker Prize-winning and 'Booker of Bookers'-winning,
best-selling novel, to which I owe an obvious debt.

The lives of those born in the first decades of a newly independent nation
were blighted by scarcity of resources, lack of opportunity, and low growth led
by largely incompetent governments. Caste- and religious-based violence was
never far away and Rushdie captured in his novel the terrible toll these took in
the three decades after 1947. Gandhi, the 'father of the nation', and two prime
ministers were assassinated and thousands died in riots. Many, my late father-
in-law Ramniklal Trivedi included, saw opportunity in foreign lands and left in
search of greener pastures. They migrated as part of an unprecedented brain
drain and built affluent lives for themselves in other parts of the world where
they contributed directly to the economic growth of other nations and indirectly to their own through the huge remittances sent back to India by the
diaspora. India languished doggedly near the bottom of the development
tables. The lure of migration, and the economic security that came with it,
over decades meant that by 2016 the Indian diaspora was the largest in the
world with 16 million people of Indian origin living in other parts of the planet
according to the United Nations (*The Times of India*, 2016).[4]

It is interesting that so many migrant Indians have been hugely successful
and they are disproportionately represented in the C-suites of many global
enterprises. Sundar Pichai at Google, Microsoft's Satya Nadella, Indra
Nooyi at PepsiCo, and Vasant Narsimhan at Novartis are a few of the
many Indian-origin CXOs running global enterprises. There seems to be
something alchemical that happens when Indians leave their county of birth
and spend time studying and working in foreign countries – particularly the
US. Alan Rosling, former Tata insider, was the first non-Indian to serve on
the board of Tata Sons, the group's holding company. Now an entrepreneur
and author, he looks at this phenomenon in his excellent recent book *Boom
Country: The New Wave of Indian entrepreneurship*. One factor he identifies in the explosion of a start-up ecosystem in India over recent years is the
influence of US-education and the experience of young Indian's who've cut
their teeth in Silicon Valley and then returned to India with entrepreneurial
spirit and new-found confidence.

Imagine what India's economic landscape might have been if for decades
such talent hadn't departed but stayed to work in an environment that was
conducive to their skills and supportive of their drive. A changing global
environment marked by low growth in developed markets and high rates in
emerging markets, including India, have resulted in a new wave of retur-
nees. Hotel-group heiress and hospitality entrepreneur Amruda Nair sees

this as the main difference between her generation of millennials and the parental generation. For her the lure of international education and work experience was not a way of migrating but a stepping stone to success on returning to India. 'Everyone wanted to go and study abroad and then maybe stay for a year or two to get experience and work with the right brands but the intent was always there to come back. That's where the shift happened', she told me. Others are returning for a combination of reasons, some familial, others professional. Most are motivated, as was I, by the uptick in opportunity enshrined in the emerging 'Asian Century'.

For the cousins, brothers, and sisters who stayed in India during those post-Independence decades there was a constant struggle for resources. Incomes were low. Life expectancy was poor. Space was at a premium. Opportunities were few and far between. A job was for life. Outside the major metropolitan centres of Mumbai and Delhi job prospects remained restricted by caste membership. Marriages were predominantly arranged and matches made along caste lines and for economic reasons.

In a richly researched and colourful archive of stories collected by the Centre for Civil Society to mark 25 years of economic reform, and presented at its website www.indiabefore91.in, visitors can read and watch vignettes that capture the sense of frustration and powerlessness and the terrible waste of talent that came from successive governments' inability and unwillingness to create an environment that fostered growth and innovation. Shreekant Gupta of the prestigious Delhi School of Economics illustrates the point with the story of CM Stephen, a Congress politician who served as a communications minister under Prime Minister Indira Gandhi. In the 1970s and 1980s it would take several years from the moment you put your name on the state monopoly's waiting list to the time you received a telephone line. The phone would then function only intermittently. Rather than acknowledging any failure on the part of government for its shoddy performance or recognising that access to even rudimentary communications tools could be a catalyst for all kinds of other economically valuable activity, CM Stephen is quoted as having said that: 'if people are not happy with their phones they can send them back'.[5] This attitude seems to capture perfectly the mix of unsound economic policy, governmental overreach, and communal fatalism that characterised the Licence Raj. Anyone over 40 years of age in India will have stories from their formative years with which to regale a guest; of standing in a queue to book a trunk phone call at the PCO to call a relative in another city; buying a Godrej cupboard because it was the only brand available; waiting expectantly when family visited from overseas with the hope that they'd bring branded products not available in India.

The nephews and nieces whom I've now known for 20 years have grown up and come of age in an India that is changed, in many ways beyond recognition. They certainly haven't had to wait for a phone connection. They can walk into a branch of Vijay Sales or Croma, India's leading electronics retailers, and pick up the latest model of their preferred brand of mobile phone. Or they can log onto Amazon, or its local rival Flipkart and, using net banking or paying via a mobile wallet, have a phone delivered the next day. A host of telecoms companies compete to sell them connectivity and a plethora of app developers provide them access to everything from personalised astronomy to investment advice. In a country that's steeped in superstition and numerology, astronomy and investment go hand in hand. Setting up their own homes, they can now choose from a massive range of furniture at online store Pepperfry rather than be forced to buy the one thing available.

The life experiences and expectations, the opportunities available to them, their life expectancy, career choices, and marriage prospects are vastly different to those of their parents and grandparents.

They, and another 440 million of their contemporaries, are Midnight's Grandchildren (Figure 1.1).

The young Indians entering the workforce now and in coming years were born after 1991. They have grown up in a country where, albeit unevenly and in fits and starts, scarcity was being replaced by relative abundance. Lack of opportunity has given way to a host of new career options. Where their parents and grandparents had made a career choice (or in reality often had it made for them) and looked forward to a steady progression in a 'job for life', time marked by a predictable and reliable succession of designation changes and salary increments, India's millennials have rather different ideas. Many are contemplating and making decisions that will lead to alternative career paths.

Where once there was a single technology provider (the phone company) these digital natives now have ready access to an almost unlimited number of devices. The same is true of jeans and sneakers, handbags and head-scarves, cars and computers, and bank accounts. The range of choices grows exponentially. No area of life has been unaffected. Entrepreneurship was an option unavailable to all but the well connected few in the era of licences and permits. Starting a business is increasingly a real and mean-ingful choice, and one that won't necessarily kill off marriage prospects as it undoubtedly did in the past.

Our business magenta is made up of Indian millennials. The conversations I overhear in the office are enlightening. Over time I became aware of some of the tensions being played out as a generation of young people left school and college, joined the workforce, became consumers, made important life decisions, and prepared to start families of their own. In my professional life

INDIA IS HOME TO

440 MILLION MILLENNIALS

Figure 1.1

I spend time with organisations that want to be better at communicating with the people that are important to them. Lots of those are large Indian companies. I see many examples where organisations are struggling to engage the young people joining the workforce and having difficulty developing brands that will appeal to them as consumers. In large part that is because the leaders and managers and policy makers in those organisations are people who are part of the earlier generations – primarily 'Gen X'ers, with several million baby boomers still hanging around waiting to retire. The systems and policies, the rituals and routines that underpin their lives were designed in and for an earlier era. A profound tension exists between the generations and it manifests itself in a number of ways. Some organisations are realising that they cannot expect to succeed by imposing a set of principles, systems, processes made during the era of scarcity economics on a generation of young aspirants. For some this has become the burning platform.

My thesis is that the delta of change – the coming of age of Midnight's Grandchildren, their graduation to employees, consumers, parents, and imminently business leaders – is unprecedented.

In western democracies there have been, since the Second World War, an ongoing series of cultural, political, and economic revolutions. Each cohort has fought its generational battles and felt it to be in the vanguard of a brave new world. In real terms the inter-generational differences have been relatively small. In India the tensions are greater as an old order struggles to remain relevant and the young fight against the traditions of centuries past. And the scale is unprecedented too. That's one of the things that makes this moment in Indian history so important and exciting. And if this is to be the Asian Century then what happens in India is important to the other five-sixths of the world's population that don't live in the country.

In her brilliant book *The End of Karma: Hope and Fury among India's Young*, Somini Sengupta captures the internal tensions that aspiration has created. 'Aspiration is a meme that infected India's idea of itself', she writes, and describes the election of former *chaiwala* (teaboy) Narendra Modi as prime minister in 2014 as the embodiment of aspiration. He won on the back of a slogan that promised 'Good times ahead' and appealed to an electorate in which 150 million were first-time voters (*The Economic Times*, 2013).[6]

The lives of the young urban Indians I describe in this book, in many ways thanks to the effects of globalisation, resemble those of their contemporaries in other parts of the developed world more so than they correlate to their peers in rural India. Theirs is a unique experience. They are grappling with a complex transition from tradition to modernity. India is on the cusp of another moment of transformation, as the post-'91 generation becomes the dominant force in the workplace, the key target segment for brands, and a political force wielding immense power.

A little over 70 years after they were spoken, Nehru's words seem to have found a new lease of life as 'the soul of a nation, long suppressed, finds utterance'.

Notes

1 *The New Yorker*, June 2015. The great divide: the violent legacy of Indian Partition. Available at www.newyorker.com/magazine/2015/06/29/the-great-divide-books-dalrymple. Accessed on 19/07/2018.
2 Manmohan Singh quoted in Goswami O, 2017. Remembering 1991 … and before, in R Mohan, *India Transformed: 25 Years of Economic Reforms*, Penguin.
3 NDTV, 2017. India will be the world's youngest country by 2020. Available at www.ndtv.com/india-news/india-will-be-the-worlds-youngest-country-by-2020-1673752. Accessed on 22/07/2018.
4 *The Times of India*, 2016. India has largest diaspora population in world, UN report says. Available at https://timesofindia.indiatimes.com/nri/other-news/India-has-largest-diaspora-population-in-world-UN-report-says/articleshow/50572695.cms. Accessed on 22/07/2018.
5 Quoted anecdotally by Shreekant Gupta at www.indiabefore91.in (accessed on 28/09/2018) and Sashi Tharoor in his book *Midnight to the Millennium*.
6 *The Economic Times*, 2013. 2014: winning India's 150 million first-time voters. Available at https://blogs.economictimes.indiatimes.com/headon/2014-winning-india-s-150-million-first-time-voters/. Accessed on 22/07/2018.

2 Why India matters

India's potential polarises opinion.

There is a ream of evidence to support the view that India has achieved much in the past 25 years. But there is much that it has failed to achieve.

In 'Changes and Challenges: Corporate India since 1991' Indian economist and journalist Omkar Goswami reports that between 31 March 1991 and 31 March 2016:

> The top-line (gross sales plus other operating income) for all listed companies was eleven times greater in 2016 than 1991. Profit after tax (PAT) was twenty-five times greater in the course of those twenty-five years. Market capitalisation was 118 times greater. Simply put, the top-line grew at 10 per cent per annum, PAT at 13 per cent, and market cap at 19 per cent. India had not witnessed such corporate growth rates – or anything remotely close – in the period between Independence and 1990.
> (Goswami, 2017)[1] (Figures 2.1–2.3)

India has undoubtedly experienced unprecedented economic growth in the past 25 years. It is also clear that the distribution of that growth has been unequal. India's much-hyped middle class remains relatively poor and has very limited discretional spending power. A quarter of a century since reforms began, many are yet to feel the benefits and remain trapped in a system that discriminates on multiple counts: gender, caste, region, colour of skin, and religion. What happens next is an important question.

Much is made of India's demographic dividend, a term coined to describe a bulge in the working age population that coincides with declining fertility rates. The numbers are staggering.

A population explosion during the decade from 1991 to 2001 saw the country's population grow by more than 182 million as it broke the billion barrier (Figure 2.4). That's the equivalent of adding around three times the population of the UK – in a decade. The population growth rate slowed a few percentage points – down from 21.5 per cent to 17.7 per cent in the decade to 2011 – but in real numbers that was still another 180 million people added.

THE TOP-LINE FOR ALL LISTED COMPANIES WAS

11 TIMES GREATER

IN 2016 THAN 1991

Figure 2.1

PROFIT AFTER TAX (PAT) WAS

25 TIMES GREATER

IN THOSE 25 YEARS

Figure 2.2

MARKET CAPITALIZATION WAS

118 TIMES GREATER

Figure 2.3

**1991 TO 2001 SAW THE COUNTRY'S
POPULATION GROW BY**

MORE THAN 182 MILLION

Figure 2.4

At present around one in every six people on the planet is Indian. Numbers will continue to rise and by 2022 the UN says India's population will overtake China's, as it becomes the world's most populous nation. By 2040 it is likely that India's population will exceed 1.5 billion (United Nations Department of Economic and Social Affairs, Population Division, 2015)[2] (Figure 2.5). Mumbai, my adopted home, is the fourth largest city on the planet (Insider Inc., 2018)[3] and is ranked one of the most densely populated.

**BY 2040, INDIA'S POPULATION
IS LIKELY TO EXCEED
1.5 BILLION**

Figure 2.5

In the 2011 census 62.6 per cent of India's 1.2 billion people were of working age defined as between 15 and 59 years. That was up to 64.4 per cent by 2015 (IndiaSpend, 2017).[4] In 2020 the median age of an Indian will be just 29 years (Figure 2.6). India is already home to 440 million millennials. Add the Gen Z cohort that follows and India has around 830 million people (Figure 2.7), more than half its population, aged less than 35 years.

One million young Indians join the workforce every month (Figure 2.9). Or they would like to if the jobs were available and they had the skills that employers look for. More than 12 million jobs have to be created every year. In 2015, then newly elected prime minister, Narendra Modi, launched Skill India, a programme whose mission is to train 'at scale, with speed and high standards' 400 million young Indians by 2020. Shoba Purushothaman is one entrepreneur who sees the skills gap as an opportunity. Her company, Hardskills, is providing an online training solution to corporations. Others will follow. As part of the education requirement an estimated 40 million new university places are needed (UKIBC, 2018).[5]

**IN 2020, THE MEDIAN AGE
OF AN INDIAN IS JUST
29 YEARS**

Figure 2.6

**INDIA HAS AROUND
830 MILLION PEOPLE
UNDER 35 YEARS**

Figure 2.7

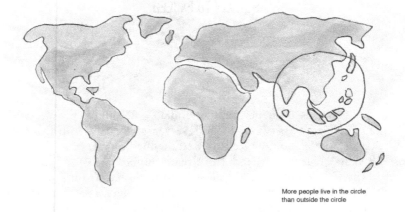

More people live in the circle
than outside the circle

Figure 2.8

MORE THAN
12 MILLION JOBS
HAVE TO BE CREATED EVERY YEAR

Figure 2.9

If these young people can be put to work they could fuel a mighty new economic advance, supercharging the development of the last quarter century, as they earn and spend. If jobs can't be created fast enough they may become a major drag on the economy. Annual job creation was reported by *The Wall Street Journal* to be at 5.5 million in 2015 (*The Wall Street Journal*, 2015),[6] well off the pace required to drive sustained growth. Indian Railways, which is ranked one of the world's top ten employers by number of employees, advertised jobs in early 2018. Media reported that it received 23 million applications for a mere 90,000 posts – more than 250 applicants per post (*Business Standard*, 2018).[7] Such numbers amply illustrate the scale of the challenge. When the Mumbai police force advertised at around the same time it received applications from many over-qualified job seekers. The 200,000 applicants for 1,137 vacancies included 3 doctors, 5 lawyers, 167 MBAs, and 423 engineers, according to the *Mumbai Mirror* (2018).[8]

GDP growth at the end of 2017 was recorded at 7 per cent, meaning India had regained its position as the fastest-growing large economy (*Financial Times*, 2018).[9] But in a country where traditional social structures are in decline and droves of young people flood to cities every day in search of jobs that don't exist, the potential for unrest, if aspirations are not met, is clear. Demographic dividend could turn to disaster.

India's young population represents at once both great opportunity and immense challenge. Finding meaningful work for these young, aspiring, and expectant millennials, who've grown up in a country experiencing rapid economic growth, rising incomes, and booming consumption, albeit unevenly distributed, is a tall order. The opportunity, assuming jobs can be created at a fast enough pace and that willing hands and minds can acquire the skills to make them employable, is that this influx of new workers will continue for the coming decades.

Many are bullish:

> The sheer size of India's youth combined with improved education paves the way for sustained growth in purchasing power and makes India's consumer story one of the world's most compelling for the next 20 years. The nation's challenge is to create enough jobs to unleash the productivity of India's youth.
>
> (Goldman Sachs, 2016)[10]

In 2011 McKinsey & Co. published a report that highlighted India's importance to the world economy in the period to 2025. Its claim was that 47 per cent of global GDP growth, US$23 trillion-worth of new GDP (Figure 2.10), in that 15-year period would come from a mere 440 emerging cities in the developing world. Many of them are in India. Places like Vadodara, Pune, Bhubaneswar, Nagpur, Ahmedabad, Surat, and Jaipur (McKinsey & Co., 2012).[11] Places very few executives have heard of, and wouldn't be able to find on a map, said the consultancy's report. I've had the chance to explore some of them and we'll meet young Indians in these vibrant urban centres in subsequent chapters.

GLOBAL GDP GROWTH
US$23 TRILLION
FROM
440 EMERGING CITIES
IN THE WORLD

Figure 2.10

Opinions on the rise of the country's middle class differ, wildly sometimes. In a 2016 report two Mumbai-based academics (Quartz India, 2016),[12] Neeraj Hatekar and Sandhya Krishnan claimed that the middle class doubled from 300 million to 600 million between 2004 and 2012. 'Middle class', for their purposes, was defined by a daily per capita spend of between $2 and $10, a basis which catches more people than most established definitions will allow. In 2015 Credit Suisse plumped for the other extreme, saying that when measured on wealth, not income, India's middle class consisted of around 26 million people. *The Economist* has held a consistently bearish view on India for the last few years. In its January 2018 cover story 'India's Missing Middle Class' the paper claims that since 1980 'India is the country with the biggest gap between the growth of income for the top 1 per cent and the growth in income for the population as a whole' (*The Economist*, 2018).[13] It points out that even spending at a level of $10 per day barely covers life's necessities and leaves little discretionary spend.

While it's widely accepted that fewer Indians now live in absolute poverty than two decades ago, hundreds of millions still are denied a decent standard of living. Vast numbers remain destitute and excluded from the promise of 'Incredible India'.

Whatever its true size there is an emerging and aspirational Indian middle class and it is exciting interest from Indian companies and inbound investors. Incomes are rising. The government claims per capita income was up 9.7 per cent in 2016/17 (HT Media, 2017).[14] That drives demand for a host of infrastructure, public goods, products, and services. Much is made of India's trillion dollar infrastructure need. There's demand for roads and airports, education, financial services, smartphones, cars, flat-screen TVs, designer brands, fast food, online shopping, and a range of luxury lifestyle items including fine wines and whiskies. India is the world's largest whisky market. In 2014 1.5 billion litres were consumed, more than three times the volume drunk in the US, which is the second largest whisky market (*Business Insider India*, 2015).[15] It is said that more Scotch is drunk in India than is produced in Scotland (Kobayashi-Hillary, 2004).[16] Beware cheap imitations.

Feature phones dominate the mobile phone market. Smartphone penetration is still relatively low but the size of the market is such that in October 2017 *The Hindu*, a daily newspaper, reported that India had overtaken the US to become the second largest smartphone market in the world (*The Hindu*, 2017).[17] China of course tops that list. There are around 220 million smartphones in India (Figure 2.11). Year on year sales for the third quarter of 2017 were up 23 per cent at more than 40 million units. The market is skewed towards 'low end' products; a state of affairs that suggests *The Economist*'s pessimism about the middle class's propensity to spend is valid. Korean manufacturer Samsung has been excellent at tailoring its products to achieve the magic mix of quality, functionality, and price for the value-oriented Indian consumer. It has the largest market share followed

IN 2017, THERE ARE

220 MILLION

SMARTPHONES IN INDIA

Figure 2.11

closely by Chinese maker Xiaomi. Apple, by contrast, has a tiny 2.2 per cent market share according to CNBC (2018).[18] In a country where per capita income in 2017/18 was just over US$1,600 (*The Economist*, 2018)[19] only those in a few affluent enclaves are willing to stump up more than US$1,000 for even the least costly iPhone.

There are other significant trends at play that contribute to India's relative importance as an economy and a market. India is urbanising rapidly but still falls behind most developed markets in terms of the percentage of people that live in cities. At the 2011 census 31 per cent of India's population was categorised as urban (HT Media, 2017).[20] The World Bank put that number at 33 per cent in 2016 (2016)[21] (Figure 2.12). In November 2012 *The Telegraph* reported that China's urban population exceeded its rural population for the first time in history (2012).[22] By comparison, in the 2010 US census more than 80.7 per cent or Americans were classed as urban (CityLab, 2012).[23] India's shift from farms and fields to cities and skyscrapers has a long way to go.

Abhishek Lodha, is the bright, young (but marginally too old to count as a millennial), US-educated managing director of Lodha Group, a real estate developer with a penchant for high-rise buildings. He claims that a further 300 million Indians will become city dwellers in the next ten years. An alternative, dystopian vision of the future centres on the threat of automation. Widespread adoption of robotics and automation could rob India of a similar number of jobs. The BBC estimates that 69 per cent of India's roughly half a billion jobs are at risk (2017).[24] That would dramatically

33%

**OF INDIA'S POPULATION
IS CATEGORISED AS URBAN**

Figure 2.12

reduce the ability of its citizens to afford housing. As ever, opinion is divided but there's seemingly no end to the appetite for investment in real estate. Cranes march across the urban landscape as low-rise housing is demolished, to be replaced by high-rise developments stretching skywards through the smog.

Other policy initiatives are reducing bureaucracy and encouraging economic activity in India. In July 2017 a nation-wide Goods and Services tax was introduced. There are refinements to be made but it has been generally well received by economists. The unexpected act of demonetisation, when by extracting the highest denomination notes (INR500 around GBP5.50 and INR1,000 around GBP11) the government took out an estimated 86 per cent of the value of Indian rupees in circulation overnight, caused major disruption and plenty of financial hardship. The jury is still out on its long-term benefits. Writing in the *Harvard Business Review* on the eve of the first anniversary of the event Bhaskar Chakravorti was scathing: 'India's demonetization debacle ought to serve as a cautionary tale for all of us', he said (*Harvard Business Review* 2017).[25] Others have been more forgiving.

Another foundation stone for future economic growth, and financial inclusion, is the introduction of a biometric identity scheme, which aims to capture data on all 1.3 billion Indians. Aadhaar, which means 'foundation' in English, is magnificent in its ambition. It was launched in 2009. The government claimed that by November 2017 more than 99 per cent of Indian residents were covered (Unique Identification Authority of India, 2018)[26] (Figure 2.13), my family and I included. Former World Bank Chief Economist Paul Romer called it 'the most sophisticated ID programme in the world' (Quartz India, 2017).[27]

India's ability to conceive and execute such large-scale initiatives is another reason why it matters. Whereas in the past it tended to play catch up by implementing ideas that had been conceived elsewhere, it is increasingly an innovator in its own right, developing solutions locally to solve Indian problems or to drive Indian growth.

As keynote speaker at the Singapore FinTech festival in November 2017 Indian Finance Minister Arun Jaitley acknowledged that each of these

LAUNCHED IN 2009, AADHAR NOW COVERS
99%
OF INDIA'S POPULATION

Figure 2.13

Figure 2.14

policy decisions had caused some short-term pain. But the government's view is that the combination of this set of interventions is 'bound to produce long-term returns as far as the Indian economy is concerned' (*The Hindu Business Line*, 2017).[28] That the Indian finance minister was invited to give such a high-profile speech in Singapore suggests that relations between the two countries are strong and India is increasingly recognised by Singapore as a regional power and counterweight to China.

The World Bank publishes an annual Ease of Doing Business ranking. Indian media got over excited when the 2018 scores were released. The country jumped 30 places (Figure 2.15) to 100th out of the 190 countries the World Bank measures. As ever, opinion is divided. According to those bullish about India's prospects it's a quantifiable vindication of the current government's pro-business agenda. Improved ease of doing business has been seen both as a way of reducing friction for domestic businesses and making India a more attractive destination for inbound investment. If the government's flagship 'Make in India' campaign is to gain traction then doing business needs to be less troublesome. Naysayers have it that the bounce in India's ranking is driven by methodology changes rather than actual reform (Scroll.in, 2018).[29]

INDIA JUMPED
30 PLACES
IN THE WORLD BANK'S
EASE OF DOING BUSINESS RANKING

Figure 2.15

This annual data forms part of any presentation I give on doing business in India. One of the points I strive to make is that India scores very well on some measures and very poorly on others. It gets a single digit placing for its protection of minority investors. It's the fourth best county in the world on that score. One of India's many ironies is that at a broader level it doesn't do well when it comes to its protection of minority communities (YKA Media, 2017).[30] It scores double digits (29th) for both getting electricity and getting credit. All other scores are above 100. At the bottom end it continues to score disastrously on the enforcement of contracts (164th) and dealing with construction permits (181st).

This data set illustrates one of the many dichotomies of India: great progress and top-decile performance on one hand and abject failure and obduracy on the other. Small islands of excellence dotted on a sea of underperformance.

As the fastest growing large economy in the world, with a government intent on boosting economic performance and making it a more attractive place for investors, India matters economically. Politically it's important too.

As China's economic and political power increases and the US steps back from its traditional role as global leader, India's role in Asia is changing. Those such as Japan and South Korea, concerned by China's regional might, see India as a counterbalance. Democracy is raucous and firmly entrenched and means even those not yet experiencing the benefits of economic growth have a voice. As the ruling Bharatiya Janata Party (BJP) found in late 2017, it's not immune to being on the end of local protest votes as happened in the state election in Gujarat. The BJP retained its grip on power but with a reduced majority as rural voters turned to the resurgent Congress Party in a state that's been a traditional stronghold for the BJP, and which incumbent prime minster Narendra Modi led for more than a decade as chief minister.

Further afield India aspires to a permanent seat on the UN Security Council, a body formed a couple of years before Indian Independence and one that fails to reflect the geopolitical realities of the 21st century. As the Asian Century unfurls India's claim will become louder and more credible.

India has been cautious, even critical, of the China-led One Belt and One Road (OBOR) initiative. Land connections to the north and sea routes around its southern tip are designed to create the world's largest economic corridor according to its Chinese promoters. India feels threatened if surrounded by Chinese influence and investments. The US$62 billion China–Pakistan Economic Corridor is a flagship OBOR project currently raising the hackles of India's intelligentsia.

Gateway House, India's leading foreign policy think tank, questions its economic logic, saying:

> But its strategic implications are clear: The investments will facilitate the Chinese military presence in Pakistan and the Arabian Sea, where

they can menace India's oil and gas imports. It also will give China and Pakistan an opportunity to play a greater role in Afghanistan and Central Asia; this, too, could hurt India's long-term strategic and economic interests.

(Gateway House, 2017)[31]

India fears that the US's withdrawal of financial support to Pakistan opens the door for the Chinese.

Environmentally India matters. It sits almost at the bottom of the Environmental Performance Index. Massive population growth and rapid economic development are not conducive to environmental wellbeing. In the biennial report by Yale and Columbia Universities and the World Economic Forum, India sits 177th out of 180 countries. Only two countries rank worse on air pollution. India's continued economic boom poses threats not only to its own population but to the wider world too since it contributes to global warming because it emits high levels of greenhouse gases. Prime Minister Modi has been a vocal advocate of renewable power and solar in particular. Investments have flowed and much progress has been made. In mid-2017 more than 30 per cent of the country's total installed power-generating capacity was renewable. One hope is that a young generation of Indians, exposed to the wider world, influenced by science rather than myth and fatalism, and more ecologically minded, will drive change. With its population still growing and demand for power rising it has a major task if it wants to become part of the solution rather than the problem.

India's soft power is on the rise. Indian food, cricket, Bollywood movies and the music that emanates from it, yoga, tantric sex, and mythology all have ardent supporters around the globe. These give it the power to influence without military might or economic leverage.

The appeal of Indian movies extends beyond the diaspora. A recent example is the massive success of top Bollywood moviemaker Aamir Khan's pictures in China. I met Taylor Lin a visiting Beijing-based executive producer, taking the pulse of India's music scene. She told me Aamir Khan's movies gross more in China than in India. It turns out that *Secret Superstar*, his latest, a tale of a burka-wearing Indian teen who dreams of pop-stardom, took US$27 million in its first weekend in China (Quartzy, 2018).[32] So while politically the two Asian super powers may be at loggerheads over disputed territory and snipe about each other's political systems, young people are watching some of the same content and quietly finding a shared interpretation of contemporary issues.

Allied to this is an emerging sense that India is not just a place that can replicate, at lower cost, what's been invented elsewhere. Increasingly it is seen as a source of ideas and new approaches. Entrepreneurship is on the rise. A vibrant start-up culture has taken root. Innovation in India is becoming more sustainable and moving beyond the 'mend and make do' approach of *jugaad* – a Hindi term used to describe low-cost 'hacks'.

Economically one of the biggest stories of the 21st century will be the growth in Asia-to-Asia, dubbed A2A, trade. By 2020 intra-Asian trade will have greater value than Asia's trade with the west (*South China Morning Post*, 2017).[33] India is only a part of that story but its significance will continue to grow.

India is a land of extremes. Enchanting and full of promise and in the same breath infuriating and seemingly doomed to fail. Can its millennials throw off the shackles of the past and write a new script, as they become the dominant group of employees and consumers? The clash of tradition and modernity, as we'll see in the next chapter, makes India a fascinating and exhilarating place to be.

Key takeaways

1 **Proceed with caution.** Post-1991 economic performance shows India can achieve ostensibly transformative levels of growth. Its politicians have not historically been impressive when it comes to distributing the rewards. The demographics suggest that if policy makers can get their act together and create the environment within which entrepreneurship and job creation flourish then India is on the cusp of a new supercharged era of growth. But it's not guaranteed.

2 **Estimates of India's middle class vary wildly.** Many reports and analysts' recommendations tend to overstate the case for an emerging middle class or to assume that its characteristics will follow trends seen in other parts of the world. India's road to growth will not be straightforward and the realities of life outside affluent urban enclaves make it a hugely challenging market. India's sheer scale, its rate of growth, and the transformations taking place make it a prize worth working for. Even niche markets in a country of 1.3 billion people can be the equivalent size of a small, developed nation's economy.

3 **Government initiatives are making it easier to do business.** Recent policy changes are reducing friction for those wanting to participate in India's undeniable (if qualified) potential. The drive to digitisation, through demonetisation and the introduction of a biometric identity system, offers significant medium-term benefits. A combination of rule changes and a sustained, if patchy, recognition of the benefits of market-led economic policy support an ease-of-doing-business agenda. The results are being seen.

4 **The 'Asian Century' is a reality.** The boom in Asia-to-Asia trade and massive regional investments in improved connectivity add momentum to powerful demographic trends. More than half the world's population lives inside the circle (Figure 2.8), and it's predominantly young people. These are the consumers of tomorrow. Whether they act in expected ways or exhibit new characteristics, Asia is the driving force of 21st-century

economic growth. India's millennial population therefore has much to offer in that context.

5 **What happens in India matters for the rest of the world.** Economically, politically, environmentally, culturally, socially the next phase of India's development will have far-ranging ramifications. There are reasons to approach with caution, but no reasons not to participate in its growth. India's millennial cohort is the largest in the world. Its attitudes will soon dominate in one of the world's largest markets of the 21st century. The ability to succeed in a massive market with high levels of complexity and ambiguity, that's changing at speed and in many directions simultaneously, will provide a framework for growth in other markets that exhibit similar characteristics.

Notes

1 Goswami O, 2017. Changes and challenges: corporate India since 1991, in R Mohan, *India Transformed: 25 Years of Economic Reforms*, Penguin.
2 United Nations, Department of Economic and Social Affairs, Population Division, 2015. *World Population Prospects: The 2015 Revision, Key Findings and Advance Tables*. Available at https://esa.un.org/unpd/wpp/publications/files/key_findings_wpp_2015.pdf. Accessed on 22/07/2018.
3 Insider Inc., 2018. The 20 most crowded cities on Earth. Available at www.thisisinsider.com/most-crowded-places-on-earth-2017-10#4-mumbai-bombay-india-17. Accessed on 22/07/2018.
4 IndiaSpend, 2017. India's demographic dividend: 64.4% youth, 27.3% children in 2015. Available at www.indiaspend.com/viznomics/indias-demographic-divi dend-64-4-youth-27-3-children-in-2015-2015. Accessed on 22/02/2018.
5 UKIBC, 2018. *India's Education Policy: Submission to the Ministry of Human Resource Development*. Available at www.ukibc.com/wp-content/uploads/2018/03/UKIBC-Education-March2018-Pages-V3.pdf. Accessed on 22/07/2018.
6 *The Wall Street Journal*, 2015. India's labor force. Available at https://blogs.wsj.com/briefly/2015/07/22/indias-labor-force/. Accessed on 22/07/2018.
7 *Business Standard*, 2018. India's job reality on board Indian Railway: 255 applicants for 1 post! Available at www.business-standard.com/article/current-affairs/indian-railway-jobs-23-million-apply-for-90000-vacancies-rrbcdg-gov-in-all-you-need-to-know-255-aspirants-for-1-seat-118042401167_1.html. Accessed on 22/07/2018.
8 *Mumbai Mirror*, 2018. Doctors, lawyers, MBAs in the race to be Mumbai police constables. Available at https://mumbaimirror.indiatimes.com/mumbai/cover-story/doctors-lawyers-mbas-in-the-race-to-be-constables/articleshow/63791555.cms. Accessed on 22/07/2018.
9 *Financial Times*, 2018. India regains title of world's fastest-growing major economy. Available at www.ft.com/content/cb5a4668-1c84-11e8-956a-43db76e69936. Accessed on 22/07/2018.

10 Goldman Sachs, 2016. The rise of India's young consumers. Available at www. goldmansachs.com/our-thinking/pages/rise-of-the-india-consumer.html. Accessed on 22/07/2018.

11 McKinsey & Co., 2012. Urban world: cities and the rise of the consuming class. Available at www.mckinsey.com/~/media/McKinsey/Global%20Themes/Urbani zation/Urban%20world%20Cities%20and%20the%20rise%20of%20the% 20consuming%20class/MGI_Urban_world_Rise_of_the_consuming_class_Ful l_report.ashx. Accessed on 22/07/2018.

12 Quartz India, 2016. 600 million people are now part of India's middle class – including your local carpenter. Available at https://qz.com/742986/600-million-people-are-now-part-of-indias-middle-class-including-your-local-carpenter/. Accessed on 22/07/2018.

13 *The Economist*, 2018. India's missing middle class. Available at www.economist. com/briefing/2018/01/11/indias-missing-middle-class. Accessed on 23/07/2018.

14 HT Media, 2017. Per capita income rises 9.7% to Rs1.03 lakh in FY17. Available at www.livemint.com/Politics/EqruCBRa2NLXByxgIJZeNL/Per-capita-income-rises-97-to-Rs103-lakh-in-FY17.html. Accessed on 23/07/2018.

15 *Business Insider India*, 2015. Indians drink way, way more whiskey than Americans. Available at www.businessinsider.in/Indians-drink-way-way-more-whiskey-than-Americans/articleshow/47802798.cms. Accessed on 23/07/2018.

16 Kobayashi-Hillary M, 2004. *Outsourcing to India: The Offshore Advantage*, Springer.

17 *The Hindu*, 2017. India now second largest smartphone market in world. Available at www.thehindu.com/sci-tech/technology/india-now-second-largest-smartphone-market-in-world/article19926744.ece. Accessed on 23/07/2018.

18 CNBC, 2018. Why Apple sells just 2.5% of India's smartphones. Available at www.cnbc.com/2018/01/29/why-apple-sells-just-2-point-5-percent-of-indias-smartphones.html. Accessed on 23/07/2018.

19 *The Economist*, 2018. Per capita income growth may fall 8.3% to Rs 1,11,782 in FY18. Available at https://economictimes.indiatimes.com/news/economy/indi cators/per-capita-income-growth-may-fall-8-3-to-rs-111782-in-fy18/articleshow/ 62383494.cms. Accessed on 23/07/2018.

20 HT Media, 2017. How much of India is actually urban. Available at www. livemint.com/Politics/4UjtdRPRikhpo8vAE0V4hK/How-much-of-India-is-actu ally-urban.html. Accessed on 23/07/2018.

21 The World Bank, 2014. Urban population (% of total). Available at https://data. worldbank.org/indicator/SP.URB.TOTL.IN.ZS. Accessed on 23/07/2018.

22 *The Telegraph*, 2012. China's urban population exceeds rural for first time ever. Available at www.telegraph.co.uk/news/worldnews/asia/china/9020486/Chinas-urban-population-exceeds-rural-for-first-time-ever.html. Accessed on 23/07/2018.

23 CityLab, 2012. U.S. urban population is up … but what does 'urban' really mean? Available at www.citylab.com/equity/2012/03/us-urban-population-what-does-urban-really-mean/1589/. Accessed on 23/07/2018.

24 BBC, 2017. Why automation could be a threat to India's growth. Available at www.bbc.com/future/story/20170510-why-automation-could-be-a-threat-to-indias-growth. Accessed on 23/07/2018.

25 *Harvard Business Review*, 2017. One year after India killed off cash, here's what other countries should learn from it. Available at https://hbr.org/2017/11/one-year-after-india-killed-off-cash-heres-what-other-countries-should-learn-from-it. Accessed on 23/07/2018.

26 Unique Identification Authority of India, 2018. State-wise Aadhaar saturation. Available at https://uidai.gov.in/enrolment-update/ecosystem-partners/state-wise-aadhaar-saturation.html. Accessed on 23/07/2018.

27 Quartz India, 2017. World Bank's top economist says India's controversial ID program should be a model for other nations. Available at https://qz.com/933907/paul-romer-on-aadhaar-world-banks-top-economist-says-indias-controversial-id-program-should-be-a-model-for-other-nations/. Accessed on 23/07/2018.

28 *The Hindu Business Line*, 2017. India set to be 'extremely attractive' place for business: Jaitley. Available at www.thehindubusinessline.com/economy/india-set-to-be-extremely-attractive-place-for-business-jaitley/article9961476.ece. Accessed on 23/07/2018.

29 Scroll.in, 2018. The 'Modi bounce': India's Ease of Business rank jumped because of methodological change, not reform. Available at https://scroll.in/article/867693/the-modi-bounce-indias-ease-of-business-rank-jumped-because-of-methodological-change-not-reform. Accessed on 23/07/2018.

30 YKA Media, 2017. Indian Muslims and their economic oppression. Available at www.youthkiawaaz.com/2017/10/why-muslims-in-india-continue-to-be-economically-backward/. Accessed on 23/07/2018.

31 Gateway House, 2017. Pakistan: a reckless mortgage, 30 November. www.gatewayhouse.in/chinese-investments-in-pakistan/. Accessed on 28/09/2018.

32 Quartzy, 2018. China's in love with a Bollywood movie about a Muslim girl's struggle to live her dream. Available at https://quartzy.qz.com/1187750/chinas-in-love-with-a-bollywood-movie-about-a-muslim-girls-struggle-to-live-her-dream/. Accessed on 23/07/2018.

33 *South China Morning Post*, 2017. Made in Asia for Asia: how the rise of its middle class is remaking the world economy. Available at www.scmp.com/comment/insight-opinion/article/2087687/made-asia-asia-how-rise-its-middle-class-remaking-world. Accessed on 23/07/2018.

3   Tradition versus modernity

Kanika Tekriwal made *Forbes Asia*'s '30 under 30' list in 2016, just two years after she founded JetSetGo, a private jet and helicopter charter business headquartered in India's capital New Delhi. Her fledgling entrepreneurial career is in part due to a health scare that changed not only her worldview but also that of her family who had other, quite different, plans for their eldest daughter. She's from what she describes as a 'traditional Marwadi family'. Marwadis trace their origins back to the northern state of Rajasthan, but as a modern-day grouping they are spread across India. They're known as a business community. While Marwadi families, or at least their male members, ran many of India's most successful post-Independence conglomerates, there's evidence that the opening up of the economy has not been favourable to their business interests (*The Times of India*, 2002).[1] This suggests that underpinnings of success in modern-day India are not the traditional strengths that sustained past generations.

Kanika is a young woman striving to carve a place for herself in a time of immense change. She tells me:

> In Marwadi families it's made clear from birth that a girl's ultimate goal is to get married. Even if she goes abroad to study the expectation is that she'll return and marry. As a result so much education goes to waste, not because the women didn't have ambition but because the pressure to conform is so great.

She describes continued pressure on her to conform – and her own innate desire to forge an alternative path for herself. Born in Bhopal in the central Indian state of Madhya Pradesh she bought time by getting her family to agree to her studying in Mumbai and then bought more time by adding a couple of years in the UK to do an MBA. She admits she didn't spend much of her time in Coventry cramming. A passion for aviation had taken hold of her and she'd wangled a chance to work in the sector learning on the job and soaking up all the experience and knowledge she could lay her hands on. Returning to India the pressure to conform and marry didn't abate. Then she was diagnosed with Hodgkin's Lymphoma. During a year recovering the idea of a charter business crystallised. 'Even if she recovers how will we get her married now?' was, she tells me, the extended family's view. So by dint of circumstance, rather than enlightenment, she says they slowly came to terms with the fact that she was going to follow her own path. The external validation of press coverage, *Forbes*-ranking, and a growing business have slowly, she says, changed her family's opinion.

Success in modern India is, for many, not just about finding an idea and developing a business model that works. Deeply rooted social attitudes must be overturned to create the circumstances to embark on the entrepreneurial journey. Tradition is never far away, even for the successful owner of a biz-jet business.

'India lives in three centuries, simultaneously', Mohandas Pai told the audience at a Gateway House conference. Gateway House is India's leading foreign policy think tank and Pai is the former CFO of tech giant Infosys, now an investor, chairman of Manipal Global Education, and always armed and ready with a combative and insightful view. My research suggests he wasn't the originator of the phrase. The actress and Bollywood doyen Shabana Azmi may have coined it first. Sadly I've not met her so I have to make do with Mohandas as my source. But, whatever the provenance, it's a neat way of thinking about what tradition and modernity mean in a nation of such diversity and complexity. The spectrum along which tradition and modernity play out is so vast that, like most things in India, it defies simple classification.

Gurgaon is a satellite city of New Delhi, built in less than two decades on the back of the country's IT outsourcing boom and the demand it created for vast acreages of office space. Spend a day roaming the glass and steel corporate towers and the manicured squares around which they stand guard and you're in no doubt this is the 21st century. Hipsters in Nike sneakers and distressed jeans share table space in Starbucks with sharp-suited men

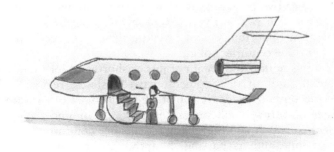

Figure 3.1

and women meeting head-hunters, real estate brokers, financial advisors, or other people's spouses. It's an e-payment funded, ride share-enabled, flat white-fuelled bubble, with Apple Watch timing. You could be in almost any central business district in the world, unless you want to use the toilet before 10am – because the facilities are outside, up two flights of stairs in the mall, and remain under lock and key until after office hours have begun. Scratch the surface and all is not quite as slick as it seems. India's leap into the 21st century is patchy.

Leave Gurgaon's gleaming steeples behind and travel on potholed roads through miles of dusty villages into the heart of India's most populous state Uttar Pradesh, and you find yourself among millions of acres of farmland. These fields are irrigated with water from the fabled River Ganges and are still being worked with equipment much as they were in the early days of the British Raj. Except that besides the ancient tools there's a very modern revolution taking place as young farmers use their smartphones to share data and receive advice about crop rotation or agri-inputs via an app developed by a new breed of agri-tech start-up such as AgroStar or RML AgTech. The latter claims to have more than 1.5 million users (*The Economic Times*, 2017).[2] Stop a while and you're transported back to a time when there was no lock on the toilet door.

Tradition and modernity bump into each other every day, in almost every aspect of life, sometimes running together in step, sometimes fundamentally at odds. A perpetual tussle is played out in innumerable places and spaces. Some tensions create new market dynamics and propel the country forward, albeit haltingly. Others have more deadly results. It's sobering to read reports in Indian newspapers of so-called 'honour killings' perpetrated within communities when couples go against tradition, defying their parents or wider kinship groups, to date or marry outside established boundaries, and pay the ultimate price. Locally elected *khap panchayats* (village assemblies) administer brutal punishments to transgressors as they have for centuries. In New Delhi and India's other mega cities such as Mumbai, Bengaluru, Pune, or Chennai, the conflicts come to a head when young migrants from traditional communities just a few hours' train ride away arrive and find themselves in close proximity to a world of wealth, opportunity, and privilege they don't recognise. The social paradigms of three centuries collide.

I've reflected on this notion and see it not just as shorthand for India's scale and the differential rates of development between states, regions, ethnic groups, and the rural/urban divide. It is that. But embedded in the idea that India lives in three centuries simultaneously is a more profound notion: that time is not a linear construct and that many Indians live comfortably with an alternate sense of time and its passing. It aptly describes Indians' highly evolved ability to deal with complexity and recognises that dichotomies and disorder are second nature. Many people comfortably manage dual realities in/out of home, in/out of work, in/out of 'real' social and 'virtual' social environments. That arranged marriage is the norm and homosexuality only recently legalised with the repeal in 2018 of Section 377 of the penal code suggests that there's been a lot of duality in many people's bedrooms too.

Daily life in India is a constant and colourful blend of tradition and modernity, each facet to be tweaked, usually in moderation and to suit the needs of the situation: traditional *salwar kameez* for dinner with parents, business suit for the office, leather jacket and hot pants for a club night; vegetarian food at home, 'non-veg' in a restaurant or someone else's residence; belief in karma and a desire to hit this quarter's targets; *puja* (prayer) in the morning, poker at night; Tinder hook-up on Friday, 'arranged marriage' date on Saturday. The list is long.

A willingness to manage those potent, sometimes contradictory beliefs or motivations is not new. It's a very traditional Indian thing. For a variety of reasons the context within which they play out is changing in essential ways. The multi-dimensional nature of tradition and modernity, the ability to blend the new with the old, to aspire while respecting the past, to live in three centuries simultaneously, is something that distinguishes millennials in India from their international peers. They live with and operate in highly complex environments. This is one of the reasons why India is simultaneously such a fascinating and frustrating place.

A brief sortie into some cross-cultural theory sets the scene for a discussion on the powerful forces both propelling and restraining, helping and hindering India's 21st-century transformation.

Hofstede's cultural dimensions

Geert Hofstede, Dutch social psychologist and Professor Emeritus of Organisational Anthropology and International Management at Maastricht University, is the originator of Cultural Dimensions Theory.

In his first iteration, published in 1980, Hofstede identified four dimensions and, like all accomplished agile practitioners, was open to refining the paradigm over time and in light of new evidence. Two additional dimensions have since been added. They allow us to define and compare cultures by measuring: Power Distance, Individualism, Feminine/Masculine, Uncertainty Avoidance, Long-term Orientation, and Indulgence vs Restraint. Originally designed to map national cultures, Hofstede went on to apply the same dimensions as the basis for defining organisational cultures. So it's possible to map India vs the UK (see below) and to map India against the culture of a particular corporate entity. Later we'll see how one multinational French company, heavily invested in India, has done just that and used Hofstede's Cultural Dimensions Theory as a framework from which to refine policies in ways that seek to close gaps between the national culture and the corporate culture.

Hofstede's theory is a convenient starting point and framework to consider India's cultural traits and idiosyncrasies. It also provides a way to

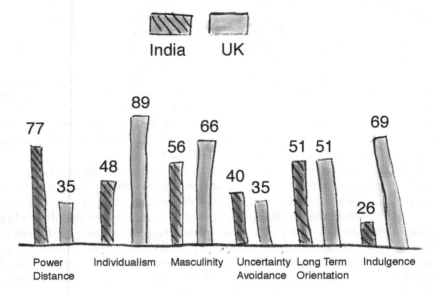

Figure 3.2 Hofstede's comparison of India and the United Kingdom

compare India with other nations that may be more familiar to us and satisfies our desire to comprehend things in relative terms.

Since this is the UK edition we'll use India/UK as a baseline for comparisons. The chart below shows the scores for each of the six dimensions. In three instances the scores are relatively close or, in the case of Long-term Orientation, identical. For Power Distance, Individualism, and Indulgence the contrasts are stark.

Power distance

This considers inequality and more specifically '*the extent to which the less powerful members of institutions and organisations within a country expect and accept that power is distributed unequally*'.

India's score on Power Distance is high at 77. In large part this stems from a traditional adherence to a strict caste system that stratified society, 'legitimised' immense inequality, and stymied social mobility. In India this high Power Distance is manifest in 'acceptance of un-equal rights between the power-privileged and those who are lower down in the pecking order'. 'Communication is top-down and directive in its style and often feedback which is negative is never offered up the ladder', says Hofstede.[3] These attitudes are entrenched in many India workplaces. Pecking orders are powerful. Status is paramount. Many offices are still carved into ghettoes of cabins with strict rules about who can sit where. Some still have separate dining rooms for executives. The flashy offices at One Indiabulls, a rare example of an iconic building among mid-town Mumbai's financial services enclave, has a lift clearly marked for 'Directors only'. A traditional observance of high Power Distance can be seen within families, in the workplace, and in a host of other institutions where strict hierarchies are the norm and respected.

The United Kingdom on the other hand has a low Power Distance score of 35. This, says Hofstede,

> exposes one of the inherent tensions in British culture – between the importance of birth rank on the one hand and a deep-seated belief that where you are born should not limit how far you can travel in life. A sense of fair play drives a belief that people should be treated in some way as equals.[4]

Individualism

India's score is intermediate, suggesting a combination of collectivist as well as individualistic tendencies. Belonging is a potent force in Indian society. Approvals are sought constantly. To be ostracised is feared and carries with it major negative implications. Family and caste connections are strong and the wellbeing and sustenance of the wider social fabric is important. And yet alongside this syndicalism sits a pervasive individualism linked to the fatalistic tenets of the Hindu faith, which rewards or punishes individuals for their deeds in a perennial cycle of death and reincarnations. As we'll see later, there's a strong case to make that, in the workplace, a focus on 'less we, more I' will encourage greater individual ownership and responsibility and that one of the important 'Jobs to be Done' by brands if they are to appeal to the millennial mindset is to enable individuality without causing offence.

In reality India is probably more individualistic than the Hofstede score suggests. It's well documented that only a tiny proportion of Indians pay income tax. In 2017 *The Economic Times* put the number at 19 million out of a population of 1.25 billion – a mere 1.5 per cent (*The Economic Times*, 2017).[5] This is in part a structural issue. All farmers are exempt, whatever their income, and a vast majority of Indians have incomes well below the tax threshold. But that shrouds a cultural phenomenon in which the needs of the group are subjugated to the highly developed individual desire to avoid paying tax. Many go to great lengths to achieve this goal.

The tax avoidance is part of a broader, firmly held belief that 'rules are for other people'. Queuing is anathema. Littering is endemic. The Highway Code is routinely ignored. No one gets anywhere on time because everyone's trying to find a shortcut. In his insightful book *The Games Indians Play* Vishwanathan Raghunathan uses Game Theory, and specifically the 'prisoners' dilemma', to unpack the reasons behind these, and other, national traits. The desire to conform kicks in when Indians travel and in foreign places they become willing adherents to local rules. That obedience

lasts until the plane touches down again on Indian soil, when the individualistic drive returns with abandon and the mad scramble to unload overhead
lockers and push past other passengers before the seatbelt sign has switched
off begins in earnest.

Meanwhile, at 88 the UK has one of the highest scores for Individualism
anywhere in the world. Individual achievement is encouraged and
applauded. Families are nuclear. British reserve and a desire for privacy
mean in many instances people don't know who lives next to them. The
British love of queuing (and expectation that others will), and long-standing
democratic institutions may suggest some counterbalance to this high level
of individualism.

Feminine/masculine

Both countries have high scores, which means they are 'masculine'. Mascu-
linity in this context is associated with competition and high performance.
Success is recognised, celebrated, and rewarded.

Ostentatious shows of wealth are common in many Indian communities,
as anyone who's had the chance to attend an Indian wedding can attest. As
a broad generalisation the further north one travels, the greater the propensity to showiness. In other communities this tendency is tempered by the
value of humility and abstinence. As Hofstede notes: 'This often reins in
people from indulging in Masculine displays to the extent that they might
be naturally inclined to'.[6]

Devotees of Jainism, an ancient Indian religious practice defined by its
adherence to a life of harmlessness and renunciation, are renowned for their
abstinence and frugality despite being an extremely wealthy business community. Parsi's are another community of highly successful business folk
with a propensity to keep their wealth hidden. While some humility is
driven by moral and religious factors, sometimes it's a more pecuniary
motivation. The exchequer's desire to track unrecorded and untaxed
income means that visible signs of opulence, such as the purchase of new
cars, may attract unwanted attention. Never judge an Indian book by its
scrappy cover!

Uncertainty avoidance

This dimension measures '*the extent to which the members of a culture feel
threatened by ambiguous or unknown situations and have created beliefs
and institutions that try to avoid these*'. A low score here signifies a culture
comfortable with ambiguity, accepting of imperfection, and willing to see
the rules bent. No surprise perhaps that India scores relatively low at 40. As
Hofstede puts it: 'It is this attitude that is both the cause of misery as well as
the most empowering aspect of the country'.[7] It manifests in various ways,
from the lax approach to time keeping and unwillingness to commit to

deadlines at an individual level to a broader collective comfort with fudge and opacity.

This has implications in professional contexts. We often find it difficult to get Indian clients to agree to a fixed and measurable set of outcomes or performance indicators. In one instance my desire to formalise a contract with a client was interpreted as a 'lack of trust' and became a major bone of contention that soured the relationship. My desire to avoid uncertainty was not reciprocated.

The UK scores 35 so has an even more relaxed attitude to ambiguity and a willingness to muddle through. These traits that deliver a low score in the Uncertainty Avoidance dimension are associated with creativity and innovation. The UK's position as a global leader in the financial services and creative industries seems consistent with this categorisation – its love of queuing an anomaly.

Long-term orientation

This dimension is a way of codifying the way cultures *'maintain links with their own pasts and manage the challenges of the present and the future'*. Both the UK and India have an identical intermediate score of 51, though there are quite fundamental differences in their respective cultures. Hofstede makes the connection between India's tryst with 'karma' and its pragmatism.

> Societies that have a high score on pragmatism typically forgive a lack of punctuality, a changing game-plan based on changing reality and a general comfort with discovering the fated path as one goes along rather than playing to an exact plan.[8]

Anyone who's had a meeting with an Indian company cancelled at no notice or, conversely, suddenly had an opportunity open up with no prior warning will understand that dynamic. We describe the result of this mentality in the phrase: 'On your marks. Get set. Wait'. An initial unbounded urgency to get moving on an initiative or project disappears as quickly as it appeared and suddenly, for reasons that are not obvious even to a trained eye, everything goes on hold while another initiative becomes of paramount importance.

By comparison, the US incidentally has a significantly lower score at 26, suggesting a culture in which short-term objectives and goals take precedence. Quarterly earnings statements, favoured by American investors, are a classic example of this short-termism and one that's been expatriated to much of the rest of the world.

Japan on the other hand has one of the world's highest scores for Long-term Orientation at 88. Japanese companies' corporate planning cycles tend to be very elongated, and far-sighted. Individual Japanese understand their life as one short moment in a very long history of mankind.

That juxtaposition between Japanese and Indian planning timeframes shows the flaw in thinking of 'Asian culture' as a common set of norms and attitudes. Some commonalities exist, but in a region that's home to more than half the world's population, there is much to differentiate.

Indulgence vs. restraint

Here we find a major divergence in the extent to which people in India and those in the UK try to control their desires and impulses. India has a low score of 26, which means it is a culture where restraint is practised. Indulgence (at least in public) is frowned upon. Restrained cultures tend towards cynicism and pessimism. Deferred gratification, the willingness to wait and see patience as a virtue, has traditionally been a feature of Indian societies. Evidence can be found in attitudes to spending and in other areas of life, such as careers.

The UK score of 69 is a sign that its people aren't great at holding back, deferring gratification, or resisting temptation. Rather they are described by their willingness to let go, enjoy life, and have fun. What's seen as 'British reserve' may be a counterweight to this tendency.

Indulgent cultures such as that of the UK are said to have proclivity towards optimism. Current reality may indicate that the reverse is true. Deloitte's study of millennials suggests that in emerging markets, including India, they are more optimistic than the better-off, but pessimistic-about-the-future western cohort (Deloitte, 2018).[9]

Hofstede's model gives us a picture of traditional India. In all dimensions, there are forces of modernity that, to varying degrees, are challenging the status quo. Power Distance is being eroded; individualism is on the rise, or perhaps there's less pretence towards collectivism; short-term gratification is becoming more acceptable. As with any change it's messy and uneven. Tensions are played out in all aspects of life.

Caste casts a long shadow

Degree-level sociology necessarily requires study of India's caste system. In that context I read theoretical descriptions by MN Srinivas and others. My understanding was abstract, rooted in ideas of ritual purity, the sacred, and the profane. Interesting but not very visceral.

It wasn't until I lived in India that I understood its pervasive and discriminatory nature. To understand modern India it's important to have at least a cursory understanding of caste and the impact it has on life chances.

The term caste, originally coined by Portuguese colonialists, has been used as shorthand for a couple of distinct concepts. Both categorise people into a hierarchy based on their occupation and status in life and dictate the ways in which their interactions are to be managed. The term *varna* originates from Sanskrit and translates as type, order, colour, or class. From this term comes a categorisation of people into four groups based on the jobs they do. At the top of the pyramid are Brahmins, the priestly caste of scholars, teachers, and lawmakers. Below them sit the Kshatriyas, the administrators, rulers, and warriors. The merchant class and agriculturalists are the Vaishyas. Shudras is the name given to the group that includes labourers and service providers. One colourful way of describing the order of the groups is to imagine them as a body with Brahmins as the head, Kshatriyas as the arms, Vaishyas, the sturdy legs, and Shudras as the feet. Outside this four-fold categorisation lie the group now known as Dalits, formerly Untouchables.

The other concept from which caste belonging is derived comes from the term *jati*. The word exists in most Indian languages and translates as 'birth'. *Jati* is distinct from *varna*, though both rely on occupation as their organising principle. *Jati* describes a more fluid and proliferate categorisation of tribes, clans, and family groupings. Some estimates put the number of *jatis* at more than 3,000 and scholars generally accept that there is a greater degree of mobility between these groups than occurs in the four-fold, *varna*-based definition of caste. Traditionally marriage within a *jati* has been the norm in India and remains so in many communities. Surnames often immediately identify an individual as a member of a particular *jati*, and Indians have an ear attuned for the information that can be gleaned simply by knowing a person's family name – the question often posed as 'What is your good name?' Increased social mobility, the move from rural to urban, a loosening of community controls, offers some the chance to jettison their caste-associated names.

At the heart of each concept is the notion that an individual is born to a group and will remain there as did his or her parents and as will his or her offspring. Sociologists tend to see caste as a more inflexible system than class is in a western context.

While caste is often described as a feature of Hinduism, other communities in the subcontinent also practise similar models of discrimination with rules applied to minimise mixing between groups and strict social policies governing interactions.

Throughout much of the colonial era the British, never averse to a bit of divide-and-rule, used caste as a matrix for allocating jobs and employed only upper castes as administrators within the Raj.

Drafted by a man born into the Dalit or Untouchable community, the Indian Constitution was introduced in January 1950. From humble beginnings, and despite obvious impediments, BR Ambedkar rose to be India's first law minister.

The Constitution outlaws the practice of 'untouchability' and makes it illegal to discriminate on the grounds of caste. At the same time it encourages positive discrimination by categorising Dalit groups as Scheduled Castes and Tribes and guaranteeing that a certain number of college places and government jobs are 'reserved' for disadvantaged groups. Some degree of backlash to this is never far from the surface of Indian political debate with groups striking and taking to the streets to push their case for special treatment and scheduled status. Much has changed in the past 70 years but as the US-based, Indian-origin author, and academic Subramanian Shankar puts it:

> Still, caste in India remains a powerful form of social organisation. It segments Indian society into marital, familial, social, political and economic networks that are enormously consequential for success. And for a variety of practical and emotional reasons, these networks have proven surprisingly resistant to change.
>
> (Scroll.in, 2018)[10]

What caste you're born into in India still has a bearing on the education you'll receive, what job you'll do, and who you'll marry. As a frame of reference it helps us understand why India is such a complexly layered society in which Indians sense of themselves is highly dependent on the need to 'belong' and to measure their value in relation to that of others. This relativism, combined with the fatalism that comes from caste and Hindu belief, is a fundamental aspect of the Indian psyche.

For a generation of young Indians the future is not ordained, destiny is not a *fait accompli* but a story yet unwritten.

Caste was a peripheral theme in my interviews and research for this book but was touched on, sometimes explicitly at others implicitly, by several of my sources.

My nephew, Kartikeya Tutwala, is one of the children I'd met on my first visit to India. He's now a young man, a city-born millennial who's developed an interest in farming and plans to set up an agri-business. To learn about agriculture and test some ideas about improved yields and better supply chains, he spent a year living in rural Maharashtra and I had the opportunity to glimpse his life there. He spoke about the degree to which caste coloured social and economic relationships in farming communities in a way that was completely unknown to him as he grew up in the melting pot of urban Mumbai. We'll hear from him in the next chapter.

Amrit Thomas explains caste and family structures as an economic reaction to scarcity and lack of opportunity:

> Family and caste systems were a response in a scarce market for economic stability. Born in a certain caste, that was your destiny. The social fabric and caste system were born to create harmony within a certain economic reality. With liberalisation that economic reality completely exploded.

Amrit is father to a millennial and professionally a seasoned sales and marketing guy who serves as CMO for the Indian arm of Diageo, the world's largest alcoholic drinks business, perhaps appropriately as his name translates as 'nectar'. Under Amrit's direction Diageo has spent time and money on appraising India's millennials and their relationships with, among other things, booze. We met, not in a bar, but in the more sober surroundings of Diageo's Mumbai office in a former mill building, where we had a working, teetotal lunch.

Amrit speaks about the loosening of rigid power structures:

> Millennials' relationship with authority figures has changed quite drama-tically. They're no longer dependent on parents and teachers, for their worldview. People who are senior, parents' friends, a cop, no longer have the same authority. In the past respect was given not earned. Now the authority figure has to earn respect and it's not just given.

As the original source of authority in any life, relationships with parents are by definition caught in this moment of change. Traditionally Indian parents have held the purse strings up to a fairly late stage in life. It's not the only lever they control but it's been a powerful deterrent and regulating force. In my professional life in India I've seen talented people forced to abandon potentially brilliant careers or loving relationships because there's pressure to join a family business or follow another path, or marry 'a suitable boy'. That force may be accompanied by threats of disinheritance. Jet-setter Kanika Tekriwal's experience, described at the head of this chapter, captures the prevailing sentiment.

But evidence suggests that family structures are changing quite rapidly in India. Urbanisation, rising incomes, better life expectancy, and western influence have all contributed to a rise in the number of nuclear families in India. The 2011 Census reported that 70 per cent of Indian households were defined as nuclear families. In fact in the preceding decade there had been a small uptick in the number of extended or 'joint families' in urban areas, possibly as an economic response to the high cost of living in cities and the lack of space. The number of rural nuclear families was on the rise (*The Indian Express*, 2017).[11] The long-term shift in household make-up, from large, multigenerational, extended or 'joint families' to small nuclear families, combined with large-scale urbanisation has changed the dynamics between generations. Elders who would have once held powerful sway, when they were a daily presence in a young person's life, are less formidable, and are robbed of influence when only seen intermittently on occasions such as Diwali or other festivals.

Amrit again:

> We've had this move from joint to nuclear family and at the same time massive and unprecedented urbanisation in search of progress and moving up the ladder. Traditional family structures that were our support systems are breaking down. The Indian solution to this challenge will be a combination of modernity and tradition, part western and part eastern. The Indian millennial mindset says this: 'I'll continue to be a respecter of tradition but I'm going to interpret it in really modern and contemporary ways so that it works for me'.

Two ideas in his last statement strike me as worth holding onto as we progress. First, the notion of 'millennial mindset' – that millennialism (which, I note, Microsoft Word accepts without hesitation as a term) is an attitude, a worldview, rather than a demographic or generational construct. I have met middle-aged Indian 'proto-millennials' with portfolio careers and greying hair. And we must acknowledge that the forces of reaction are also powerful and there are many who have vested interest in seeing tradition upheld. Some of those reactionary forces are supported by groups of Midnight's Grandchildren. Millennials are not the only modernisers and not all millennials are modernisers.

Second, the respect for tradition while interpreting it in modern and contemporary ways is perhaps the essence of Indian millennials. Hybrids emerge to achieve this balance. Success in India cannot be achieved without an ability and openness to finding uniquely Indian 'interpretations' to challenges. India is comfortable with ambiguity and can tolerate high levels of uncertainty, adapting rather than adhering to a rigid plan. Localised, hybrid solutions are emerging, not just in family institutions but also in other areas of life.

The case of McDonald's is instructive. In most of the world it's known for selling beef products. In India approximately 80 per cent of the population are Hindus, for whom the cow is sacred, and around 30 per cent of people are vegetarian. So McDonald's success is remarkable and can be attributed to its readiness to adapt its product offering to local tastes. It's an example of the success of hybridity. Where else in the world would you find a chicken burger branded a Maharaja Mac? But it is much more than just re-branding a chicken sandwich that marks the company's success. In some places it offers vegetarian-only menus and caters to other whims such as serving Jain items to satisfy the strict dietary demands of this religious community that won't eat anything that's grown underground – so no potato, onions, or garlic. McDonald's has been outstanding at localising and finding uniquely Indian solutions.

Almost two decades ago two of my friends took a year off from their London jobs to travel the world. Having spent months trekking in Nepal and northern India they landed in New Delhi. In Connaught Place, the epicentre of the capital's concentric design, they succumbed to temptation and headed into McDonald's in search of an alternative to *dal* (lentils) and rice. The only Caucasians in the queue, they fell into conversation with a young Delhiite. He was pleased they were enjoying a quintessentially Indian dining experience and surprised, but delighted, to hear that there were branches of McDonald's in their home city. This was to his mind a great example of India's expansion into the wider world. So well had the burger company localised its offering that he believed it was an Indian brand. Of course in the days of Instagram and Snapchat, where every meal is photographed and posted online, it's unlikely that anyone would be under that illusion now. It's a powerful illustration of how unlikely unions can be

Figure 3.3

formed when there's a willingness to recognise local requirements. McDonald's has made itself part of the ecosystem in urban India despite the apparent obstacles (Figure 3.3).

Arranged marriages still hold sway

Globally more than 50 per cent of all marriages are arranged and the divorce rate among arranged marriages is 6.3 per cent. In India arranged marriages still account for more than 85 per cent of weddings according to Statistic Brain (Statistic Brain Research Institute, 2018),[12] which puts the divorce rate of Indian arranged marriages at a meagre 1.2 per cent.

A Suitable Girl, a 2017 Tribeca-festival award-winning documentary, made by two foreign-born women of Indian origin, looks at the lives of three middle-class millennial Indian women as they navigate the process of finding a partner. Despite education and successful careers, and the financial independence that comes with that, they still find themselves drawn to arranged relationships rather than the alternative of a so-called 'love marriage'.

Speaking to *The Washington Post* the movie's co-director, Smriti Mundhra, said:

> I really began to understand why young people in India overwhelmingly opt-in to the system. I think it comes down to a sense of belonging. ... Being

a part of a larger community does provide support, sustenance and meaning. In India, marriage is key to belonging in society.

(*The Washington Post*, 2017)[13]

'Belonging' remains a powerful force in Indian society even at this moment of flux. It offsets desires for independence. The knack in engaging Indian millennials then is to find that balance, to allow them to find autonomy without fear of being ostracised.

With origins in the early 20th-century sociology of Max Weber, Modernisation Theory predicted that, as traditional societies evolved, they would discard age-old practices such as the arranged marriage model. It would be replaced by more western-style marriage and that the average age at marriage would increase as industrialisation and urbanisation took hold (Wiley Online Library, 2016).[14] The median age of marriage has increased slightly in India in the recent decades. In the 2011 Census it was reported to be 22.8 years for men and 19.2 for women (*Outlook India*, 2017).[15] Levels of education play an important role. The better educated wait longer to marry. But the involvement of parents in the choice of partner persists, largely with the approval of those to be betrothed. In 2013 an IPSOS poll stated that 74 per cent of Indians aged 18–35 would prefer their parents to choose their life partner (Cultural India, 2018).[16] Given the low divorce rates ascribed to arranged marriages one could say there's empirical evidence to support their view. The reality is that while divorce is still taboo and many will stay in an unhappy marriage rather than suffer the ignominy of a 'failed' union, women's lack of economic independence in India is also a major contributor to low divorce rates.

This strong, continued bias towards traditional marriage patterns suggests that while many aspects of life in India have followed an evolution seen in more modern, western societies, India is experiencing a hybridisation rather than a unilateral shift.

The dating game

Some of India's urban millennials increasingly conform to the stereotype that, like their international peers, they spend their time in cars they've booked on Uber travelling to meet people they've hooked up with on Tinder to 'Netflix-and-chill'. And when they're done with that they'll order take-out food via a delivery app and transact using a mobile-enabled payment wallet. The platforms may change between regions but similar stories are being played out in Miami, Munich, Mombasa, and Melbourne.

What is uniquely Indian is the ease with which they manage that chance of instant gratification without turning their back on tradition. Many are comfortable to hook up with someone they met on Tinder on a Friday night

Figure 3.4

and then see an 'arranged marriage boy', introduced through a family connection and pre-approved by the parents, on a Saturday. Step into a branch of Café Coffee Day in any Indian city on a Saturday afternoon and you'll find dozens of such meetings. Coffee is peripheral to the experience. Indian millennials seem open to finding a life partner through either route and will keep their options open (Figure 3.4).

In reality Tinder is just a modern version of what's been going on for (more than three) centuries in India, where the passing around of bio data – including details of birth time, alignment of the stars, height, weight, caste origins, parental employment, and even skin tone – is standard practice. In the past there would have been paper versions and even column inches in the matrimonial section of a newspaper. Then came websites such as shaadi.com. Now the same information buzzes through a messaging service and does the rounds of friendship groups; rejected by one, passed on to another.

So the principle of 'swiping' one way or the other is not new. Technology is disrupting the age-old dynamic because it puts the swipe firmly in the hands of young people and allows them to circumvent the prying eyes of parents and a battalion of 'aunties' whose most important missions in life include matchmaking.

These changes are being reflected in popular culture. The mobile phone lets boys and girls, men and women speak to each other in ways not previously possible, and to individuals not previously known. It has been a great enabler and disruptor on many levels. The ubiquity of the mobile phone sparked a fad of pop songs in local languages. Many were themed around 'the missed call', a trope in modern India that signifies a host of new opportunities. In the Hindi pop song of that name we hear from the woman's perspective the anticipation and delight in finding out who the secret admirer is. In advertising it's morphed into an active customer engagement tool – give us a missed call and we'll get back to you – say several brands.

Spending habits being disrupted

However the unions are fashioned, the economics of family units formed after marriage are changing. Living in large multigenerational families, young adults often found themselves in rent-free accommodation with their daily needs taken care of. Thus, while their individual incomes may have been low, small outgoings meant there was money left over for other purchases. In nuclear families a larger proportion of income is allocated to accommodation and subsistence costs such that the absolute amount left for discretionary spending may be lower. The real estate developers' gain may be the travel agents' or the smartphone retailers' loss.

As incomes rise and new purchasing opportunities present themselves, spending patterns are changing. As millennials earn and take financial control of their own lives, traditional models are coming under pressure. Customarily in Indian families large proportions of income were saved. That's historically been given as a reason for underinvestment, because money that could have been oiling the wheels of the economy has been stashed away in bank accounts, under mattresses, or converted into gold, a traditional way of saving for important events including children's education and weddings. But gross domestic savings rates are in decline. Indians save less now than they did a generation ago.

Several factors are at play. Traditional endorsements on spending are loosening as relationships with authority become disjointed; credit, once deemed socially undesirable, is becoming more widely acceptable and readily available; and India's millennials, like their international counterparts, are more open to a rent-not-buy model where they'll spend money on experiences rather than assets.

Ad agency boss Mahua Hazarika explains to me how many young Indians now see money more as a resource that can be repeatedly deployed to achieve experiences, rather than something to be sunk into an asset. She believes the traditional sanctions on spending are fading. A straight-talking Bengali born in Calcutta (now Kolkata), she splits her time between the offices of Rickshaw in Mumbai and Delhi. Perched in a small, glass-walled office overlooking the creative studio below she exudes (occasionally profane) enthusiasm.

She describes the shift in consumption patterns in the context of what she describes as the Brahminical nature of spending in traditional Indian communities:

> There was a lot of spending but it had to be sanctioned. I could spend vast sums on rituals such as marriages and births and religious festivals so long as it had been preordained. As relationships with authority have morphed, that sanction is disappearing. So, what happens? Now I can spend the money how I want to. But the relativism of living up to the Mehta's remains! There are regional

differences for sure. I think the sanction remains stronger in south India but I see it loosening in rural India.

To illustrate the point she tells me she has a retail client that's spending money advertising in semi-rural areas where it has no physical presence outside cities such as Indore and Nagpur, on the premise that it can pull people into those larger, fast-evolving, and affluent conurbations.

> Once they arrive, they're avid shoppers. These rural consumers have access to the same content so they see the same advertising and they know the brands. In response you're seeing new distribution models arriving that may include incentivising them to travel to the brand rather than the brand being present with them.

Another factor, worth exploring when considering what's driving the shift in spending is the growing availability of credit and its ability to accelerate purchasing decisions. Jonathan Bill is a former telecoms executive and like me an India migrant, married to a UK-born daughter of East African Gujaratis. He came to India with Vodafone in 2011 and then left to become a digital entrepreneur. His focus is on using technology to 'formalise the informal'. He's ridden the wave thus far, having already exited one start-up, and now has backing from India's billion-dollar unicorn Paytm, which is itself funded by Alibaba. CreditMate, the business he co-founded with Ashish Doshi, Aditya Singh, and Swati Ladd, has pioneered lending in the second-hand motorcycle market, using some quite clever data analytics – and an old-fashioned handshake. The approach disrupts two traditional tenets of India's purchasing mentality. First, buying on credit was socially unacceptable and in an economy with very high levels of saving there were other ways to fund purchases. Second, an inherent lack of trust, and the absence of market intermediaries, the kind that publish reliable valuations or bring buyers and sellers together, compounded a mentality that buying pre-owned products was too risky.

Indian banks are at once highly risk-averse and profligate in their lending. They are overly cautious about loans to individuals, even those hypothecated against an asset. Bank employees are held in esteem, and as authority figures their proclamations are rarely challenged. At the same time they too easily fall under the spell of seemingly successful businessmen and politically connected hotshots who routinely borrow on fraudulent claims. Nirav Modi, a chain of upmarket jewellers, was outed in early 2018 as the latest in a long list of scammers.

CreditMate has been successful, particularly in communities where traditionally lenders have feared to tread. Using a credit-worthiness check that uses data but blends it with some human interactions to sift out high-risk applicants, the company has defaulting rates that are a fraction of what a mainstream lender would work on. In part that's because the stigma of being ostracised remains a powerful trigger in what are still close-knit communities. So tradition and the threat of censure continue to play a role in the success of a very new-age business.

The purchase of a motorcycle is typically an enabler of other economic benefits. Mobility improves productivity. A small business owner can cover more ground on a motorcycle than they could on a bicycle. It means he or she spends less time struggling with unreliable public transport. A person new to purchasing on credit that uses a CreditMate loan begins to build a credit history which further down the line mean access to funds for a car, a house, or a business loan.

Furthermore, like their contemporaries in other parts of the world, Indian millennials' spending habits show a willingness to indulge in immediate gratification rather than defer and to invest in experiences rather than assets. Increased internet penetration, up from 8 per cent in 2010 to almost 25 per cent in 2016 according to consultants BCG (2017),[17] provides new channels and greater opportunities to consume. Renting an apartment has become more prevalent as internal migration has created increased demand for accommodation that may not be permanent. Rather than wait for years to accumulate a deposit and secure a home loan, a greater number of young people are renting. Online furniture store Pepperfry lets you rent beds, sofas, and dining tables. Mahindra Adventure offers the thrill of off-road driving without the outlay of buying a 4×4. Streaming music services, whether localised versions of Apple's iTunes or indigenous products such as Gaana and Saavn, are blossoming.

In Chapter 6 we'll look at some of the brands that have captured millennial mindshare and are delivering products, services, and a customer experience that appeals to these new consumers for whom optimism and opportunity are more important than loyalty. Using 'The Theory of Jobs to be Done' as a lens, we'll discover that in many instances the real task is to meet the psychosocial needs of a group grappling to finding its identity and for whom modernity means autonomy and a break from the authoritarian structures of the past.

That desire for autonomy plays out in the workplace. India's middle managers are having a tough time – at home and in the office. For many Indians above the age of 35, born into the era of austerity and scarcity, career was an anchor, a place of relative surety in a world of uncertainty. The 'employee experience', as we might now think of it, was hardly inspiring. Slow but predictable progress up the ladder of corporate life, with the comfort of bigger designations and the security of annual increments, provided social standing. Now, their millennial children are 'rebelling' at home: less beholden to tradition, demanding greater freedoms, seeing a multitude of unprecedented opportunity. And in the place of work, once a sanctuary to which they could escape the uncertainties of daily life, they find similar challenges as their younger charges turn their backs on tradition, demand faster career progression, and exhibit a perceived lack of loyalty. In Chapter 5 we return to Hofstede's Cultural Dimensions Theory to explore the clash of tradition and modernity in the workplace.

Retreat from public spaces

For some concluding thoughts on the transition from old to new I turn to Naresh Fernandes, journalist, author, and jazz aficionado. Naresh is the co-author of a coffee-table book, *Bombay Then, Mumbai Now*, which captures in words and pictures the changes in the physical environment of India's commercial hub over the past century. In his more recent book, *A City Adrift*, he presents a biography of Mumbai through a more contemporary lens. One theme is what he describes as the retreat from public spaces. It's a recurrent thread as we sip stove-top espresso among the piles of books and old jazz LPs that stand unruly guard across the floor of his airy Bandra apartment where Salman Rushdie himself was a recent guest. The slow buzz of the overhead fan and the honk of traffic three floors below are drowned out by a booming baritone that matches his imposing physical presence:

> Liberalisation has had an impact in many realms and the built environment is one. Since 1991 we've seen a change in the planning regulations that allow developers to build higher walls. In the past we had low walls and our buildings had balconies and those things encourage a sense of community. One of the changes has been the rise of the gated community, the ability for the wealthy to shut themselves off from the rest of the world.

A desire to cut oneself off from the crush of humanity, whether by retreating behind the high walls of the gated community or using private rather than public transport is a feature of aspirational modern India.

It's not just the rise of these introversions that distresses Naresh but also the homogeneity of contemporary urban architecture that he sees aping western styles suited to different climates.

> Our public buildings such as train stations were distinct. What was Victoria Terminus [now Chhatrapati Shivaji Terminus at the conclusion of the Harbour Line in Mumbai] couldn't have been built anywhere else. That reinterpretation of gothic style in an Indian vernacular is unique. If you visit the new international airport [incidentally also named after the same 14th-century Maratha warlord Chhatrapati Shivaji], you could be anywhere in the world. You see it in the glass curtained high-rise buildings. In European countries they are a way of letting in sunlight, which is a scare commodity. We have no shortage of sunlight in India. All we do by creating glass towers is increase the demand for air conditioning!

Naresh draws a comparison between the homogeneity of post-1991 building design in India and its young people: 'a red-velvet-cupcake generation that wants to do things on their own terms but lacks the impulse to truly imagine a new world'.

Are India's millennials then warriors of a bold, bright future, ripping up the traditional rulebook to take control of their own destinies? Or a generation of entitled clones obsessed with posting their confectionery choices on social media?

Key takeaways

1 **Living in three centuries simultaneously has multiple meanings.** To understand the unique experience of India's millennials think about their existence in a culture where living with contradiction and complexity and finding harmonious balance come quite naturally. This concept describes a willingness and ability to comprehend life and its progress in non-linear ways. Acceptance of one idea, such as arranged marriage, is not at the expense of another seemingly incongruous one, such as the use of a dating app or the desire for greater independence. Both can coexist. Accept that duality is an important aspect of the Indian psyche.

2 **Belonging is a powerful motivator.** Many young Indians are reimagining their place in the world, but they are not jettisoning the past. The Indian millennial mindset is hungry to achieve much that is deemed modern. Modernity is at the heart of aspiration. Independence and autonomy are sought after as part of that perceived modernity, but not at the expense of a place in the bosom of family and community. Much fear is associated with the notion of being outcast. Rebellion is rare. The desire for acceptance in most cases overrides the wish for autonomy. Young Indians are highly skilled at finding equilibrium of the old and the new without overstepping the bounds. When embracing new ways of living, many find it comfortable to conform to a new set of 'acceptable' peer-approved rules. Recognise the need to belong and support it.

3 **Hierarchies are part of India's DNA.** The caste system may have been outlawed, and its grip on relationships and employment opportunities, for example, may have weakened. This is more so in urban areas than rural ones. But however couched, the notion of status – my place in relation to others – remains a highly durable force in Indian society. Deference – to elders and to those seen as holding authority – pervades every area of Indian life. It is a defining characteristic of roles and relationships in the family, workplace, and all other institutions. Approaches that challenge hierarchy may prove difficult to implement and will be met with strong resistance.

4 **Spending patterns are changing.** Constraints on spending are loosening, sporadically. This is in part driven by increased affluence and therefore the ability of more people to be consumers. It also reflects changes in familial and other authority structures and a partial weakening of traditional methods of control. Those changes are still nascent and the views of other 'stakeholders', such as family members, can be important considerations in buying decisions. Remember that much of India's financial decisions are still made communally – and that individuals therefore lack skills and reference points from which to make informed decisions.

5 **Hofstede provides a useful starting point.** Cultural Dimensions Theory provides a framework to appreciate what characterises traditional India and how it's changing. As a frame of reference – particularly as a way of measuring Indian culture against that of another nation, or a corporate entity – it offers much. When seeking to understand behaviours or attitudes it provides a way of finding the overlap or discrepancy thereby finding points of common understanding or identifying the places where greater effort may be needed to find consensus. Use it as a map to plot the journey from tradition to modernity. Don't be afraid to customise the model.

6 **Hybrid solutions are important.** India's scale and complexity means it will increasingly require and favour solutions tailored to its distinct needs. Those needs will vary between different regions and different communities. In some the pull of tradition remains more powerful that in others. While western constructs and ideas are often admired and aspired to, cut and paste approaches developed elsewhere may well fail to gain traction if they don't properly recognise the unique Indian context. The changes taking place in India are on an unprecedented scale. In many instances, therefore, there exists no roadmap or frame of reference within which to model a solution. This leaves a lot of room for innovation to respond to specific local situations and needs.

Notes

1 *The Times of India*, 2002. Marwaris losing business acumen. Available at https://timesofindia.indiatimes.com/city/kolkata/Marwaris-losing-business-acumen/articleshow/9005397.cms. Accessed on 23/07/2018.
2 *The Economic Times*, 2017. Millennial farmers log on to apps for a better yield. Available at https://economictimes.indiatimes.com/small-biz/security-tech/technology/millennial-farmers-log-on-to-apps-for-a-better-yield/articleshow/60850440.cms. Accessed on 23/07/2018.
3 Hofstede Insights. Available at www.hofstede-insights.com/country-comparison/india,the-uk/. Accessed on 28/09/2018.
4 Hofstede Insights. Available at www.hofstede-insights.com/country-comparison/india,the-uk/. Accessed on 28/09/2018.

 5 *The Economic Times*, 2017. Why income tax payers in India are a small and shrinking breed. Available at https://economictimes.indiatimes.com/news/economy/policy/why-income-tax-payers-in-india-are-a-small-and-shrinking-breed/articleshow/56929550.cms. Accessed on 23/07/2018.
 6 Hofstede Insights. Available at www.hofstede-insights.com/country-comparison/india,the-uk/. Accessed on 28/09/2018.
 7 Hofstede Insights. Available at www.hofstede-insights.com/country-comparison/india,the-uk/. Accessed on 28/09/2018.
 8 Hofstede Insights. Available at www.hofstede-insights.com/country-comparison/india,the-uk/. Accessed on 28/09/2018.
 9 Deloitte, 2018. The Deloitte millennial survey 2018. Available at www2.deloitte.com/global/en/pages/about-deloitte/articles/millennialsurvey.html. Accessed on 23/07/2018.
10 Scroll.in, 2018. Does the US have a caste problem? An Indian scholar thinks so. Available at https://scroll.in/article/866742/united-states-has-a-class-and-race-problem-and-it-may-have-a-caste-problem-too. Accessed on 23/07/2018.
11 *The Indian Express*, 2017. Rural India starts to go nuclear, urban families grow in shrinking space. Available at http://indianexpress.com/article/india/rural-india-starts-to-go-nuclear-urban-families-grow-in-shrinking-space-4737882/. Accessed on 23/07/2018.
12 Statistic Brain Research Institute, 2018. Arranged / forced marriage statistics. Available at www.statisticbrain.com/arranged-marriage-statistics/. Accessed on 23/07/2018.
13 *The Washington Post*, 2017. India has changed a lot in 70 years: but arranged marriage remains the norm. Available at www.washingtonpost.com/news/soloish/wp/2017/05/02/india-has-changed-a-lot-in-70-years-but-arranged-marriage-remains-the-norm/?utm_term=.b4d4e78e2c2a. Accessed on 23/07/2018.
14 Wiley Online Library, 2016. The decline of arranged marriage? Marital change and continuity in India. Available at http://onlinelibrary.wiley.com/doi/10.1111/j.1728-4457.2016.00149.x/full. Accessed on 23/07/2018.
15 *Outlook India*, 2017. Average age for marriage in rural and urban india gone up, says govt. Available at www.outlookindia.com/newswire/story/average-age-for-marriage-in-rural-and-urban-india-gone-up-in-last-10-years-says-govt/972384. Accessed on 23/07/2018.
16 Cultural India, 2018. Arranged marriage. Available at www.culturalindia.net/weddings/arranged-marriage.html. Accessed on 23/07/2018.
17 BCG, 2017. The new Indian: the many facets of a changing consumer. Available at www.bcg.com/en-in/publications/2017/marketing-sales-globalization-new-indian-changing-consumer.aspx. Accessed on 23/07/2018.

4   Midnight's Grandchildren

Millennials have become something of a cartoon myth. In the mainstream press (still dominated by Gen Z executives and technicians) they tend to be portrayed like minions, the stars of the *Despicable Me* movie franchise, endowed with no individual defining characteristics. Clubbed together as a uniform group they're all tarred with the same brush.

We rebuke them for being an entitled group that lacks loyalty. A 'me, myself, and I' generation that won't stick at things. In constant need of social media validation. A 'selfie' generation; life measured in 'likes' and 'retweets'. Castigated for their wish for instant gratification and their short-termism. We're told they're unwilling to put in the time and effort required to achieve career success, always on the hunt for shortcuts. No respect for tradition. Easy-come, easy-go. Marketing executives are developing personas to capture every subset and finding they're a gadfly generation with no fidelity to brands. Snowflakes that can't take criticism because of the mollycoddling. In China the term is 'strawberry' because they're 'soft and easily bruised'. Author and YouTube sensation Simon Sinek blames a faulty education system that gave kids prizes for coming last and flawed parents who told their progeny they could be anything they wanted when the real world's not like that. Their self-esteem is broken, he says. American youth in the 1950s disparagingly labelled 'teenagers' must have heard the same recriminations. With no recourse to social media they invented rock'n'roll, and sex, instead.

And yet, at the same time this young cohort finds itself heralded as the vanguard of a new world order, the denizens of the digital economy. They thrive on ambiguity and can navigate the radical disruptions swirling around them. In truth they have no choice. They are the harbingers of doom for traditional business models. Digital nomads rewriting the terms of engagement. Citizens of the sharing economy. Commercialising their social media followings and conjuring new business models. Redefining gender. Oozing self-esteem. Unencumbered by the past.

In developed economies the generation is realising that the post war social contract that promised they would be better off than their parents has failed them. But their economic contribution is necessary to meet the retirement costs of an ageing population. Few can afford to own their own homes so they end up living at home into their thirties.

In emerging economies they're full of optimism. 'Flat World' economics and the earning power of massive, young working populations propel (some of) them into the global consuming class.

In India they've been pumped full of testosterone. Trumpeted as a 'gilded generation'. Brought up to believe that because of their sheer numbers they'll power a new era of growth that will launch India into the big league. Twenty-five years of rapid economic growth has fuelled their aspiration. They will be better off than their parents. Their life expectancy will be greater. The opportunities available to them are unprecedented. They still live at home in their thirties, but for different reasons.

Tier 2 cities revving up

Rakshit eloped with his college girlfriend because her father wouldn't tolerate their 'love marriage'. They're both from the northern state of Gujarat. He's Hindu and a Patel, a surname that traditionally signifies a village leader in rural India. She's a Shah from the Jain community. While his parents had a love marriage and were willing to accept his choice, her parents were not and expected her to fall in line with their choice of bridegroom and an arranged marriage. The scenario is not uncommon in India. Jain families tend to be long on convention and want to see their offspring marry within the community. Often wealthy traders, Jains can use financial pressure, including disinheritance, as a tool of control. To sidestep those expectations requires bravery.

Rimpal's father wouldn't budge so the young lovers, who met while studying Commerce, left their respective homes and moved to Vadodara. Rakshit previously worked for ICICI Bank, India's third largest bank by market capitalisation. His father was also a bank employee, his grandfather a farmer. Over the years since Independence the family has been part of the mass migration from rural to urban India. By eloping 27-year-old Rakshit had to give up his job with ICICI where he managed gold loans – a massive business in India where vast wealth is kept as bullion. Gold jewellery is often pawned to meet family expenses such as weddings. He's now a relationship manager for CreditMate, the second-hand bike loan business co-founded by former telecoms executive Jonathan Bill.

The stakes are high for Rakshit and Rimpal. By turning their backs on tradition and embracing modernity, they've cut themselves off from family support (she still has contact with her mother and sister but not her father). They have to make their own way, without the safety net of familial networks, to achieve their goals of owning a house and having children. Rimpal plans to rent a shop and start a business that sells cutlery. They're coming to terms with the (relatively) faster pace of city life and are excited by its possibilities.

McKinsey reckoned that almost 40 per cent of global growth in the 15 years from 2011 would come from 400 cities in emerging markets. They were described as 'middleweight' cities. Populations vary from a little under one million people to more than two million. Vadodara (formerly Baroda, capital of a princely state in Gujarat) is one of them. Along with other Indian conurbations, such as Pune, Nagpur, Bhubaneswar, Lucknow, and Ahmedabad, they are often described as Tier 2 cities. I think of them as two-wheeler cities. Travel on their roads and you'll find yourself swept along in a swarm of scooters and motorcycles. It's mayhem. India overtook China to become the world's largest market by volume of two-wheeler vehicles in 2017 with 18 million new vehicles bought in that year (*The Times of India*, 2017).[1] In total there are estimated to be more than 200 million two-wheelers on India's roads. Growth in the second-hand market has been impressive in the past few years, signalling a shift in traditional highly risk-averse buying attitudes.

These cities are exhilarating, sometimes overwhelming, places with huge young populations with rapidly rising incomes that fuel demand for a host of products and services. Rents and property prices are low so the proportion of incomes that are disposable is relatively high. They are magnets for aspiring young men and women from their surrounding towns and villages. For CreditMate, where Rakshit manages relationships with a half-dozen motorcycle dealers, Vadodara is an important market.

To understand the growth potential of India and its mass-market millennials one has to get under the skin of Vadodara and similar cities.

I join Jonathan Bill (CreditMate co-founder) and Bimal Bhatt (national dealer manager), on the 12009 Shatabdi Express. On reclining seats, in a spacious and pristine air-conditioned carriage, we're served chai and omelette as the train pulls out of Mumbai Central at 6.25 am. Dawn breaks as we speed past the corrugated slums and glass skyscrapers of Mumbai's northern suburbs. The 12009 service is a commuter train. Well-shod business people sit comfortably alongside wedding-bound families, headed along the almost 500 km route to Ahmedabad. Some jump off at Surat or Baruch, briefcases in hand. A little over four hours after departure we disembark at Vadodara where porters in red shirts lug the wedding-goers' suitcases to waiting Toyota Innovas and a yellow-shirted squad of station cleaners keep the platforms in impeccable order. Sadly, though not surprisingly, the streets outside haven't benefitted from the same cleanliness drive.

Rakshit is there to meet us in his CreditMate T-shirt and is sat astride his Honda Activa – the best-selling scooter in the market. We've joined him for a tour of dealerships. Dodging the unruly hordes of two-wheelers we make our way through Vadodara and watch him meet dealers in dusty back-street showrooms. He's at ease and the dealers have positive feedback to offer. He's embarking on a new adventure, but all agree he has the skills to make it in the city.

Then we meet a new customer whose credit application is being approved that morning. In new crimson All Stars and an Adidas T-shirt, Jignesh 'Jay', a 20-year-old student is having his loan approved on the basis of his father's earnings from his job as a chef. He hadn't expected to be greeted by the loan company's CEO. Unfazed, he signs his papers on the Formica table of a Café Coffee Day, a 1,500-store chain that resonates with India's mass-market young, who gather frequently to chat over cheap, decent, coffee and snacks away from prying parental eyes and ears.

With a Rs40,000 (GBP450) loan Jay will soon be the owner of a two-year-old 150 cc Yamaha R15, a sports bike that will, he says, outdo and impress his college mates. He hopes to get it in red to match his sneakers. He's atypical of CreditMate's customers, significantly younger than the average age of just over 30 years. He speaks Gujarati but has a strong enough grasp of English to fill out the loan application forms. He's in the second year of a three-year Bachelor of Commerce degree, no specific career plan, as yet, but already on the side has a small photography business. The owner of two Canon cameras, which he rents out, he and his friends do good business photographing couples before their weddings. Early morning and at sunset at coastal sites and heritage buildings across India you can see numerous couples dressed for the occasion, having sets of photos taken. Since wedding-related expenditure gets societal sanction he's tapping a rich seam of revenue. He's already been to Mumbai and Goa for professional shoots.

The fact that there's parental approval of the loan and that his social standing is tied to his ownership of the bike, and by extension his continued ability to service the loan, means Jonathan is confident there'll be no default. He tells me:

> We're using technology to enable the application process and identify risk and to some degree strip out the running around of paperwork. But, I still believe meeting the customer and getting a physical signature is an important way of building commitment into the transaction. At the same time we're banking on the social capital that's being invested, within the family and the friendship group.

Bimal adds a comparison between Vadodara and another fast-growing city, Pune, where he says compliance rates are less impressive.

> In cities like Vadodara where community is strong and families are well established you find a very powerful motivator for that debt to be repaid. In a city such as Pune, you have a more transient community, people who've come to study, for example, or who come into the city from outlying areas to buy a bike. The social contract there is less forceful.

Figure 4.1

Impatient to get going, floppy quiff bouncing, and the prospect of a shiny new babe magnet within his imminent grasp, Jay is Indian millennial aspiration personified. With parental support he's building a credit rating for himself and well on his way to joining the consuming class. *The Economist* may be dubious about the scale of India's middle class but the reality on the ground is that, whether documented or not, in bike dealerships and coffee shops in emerging cities across India there are millions of Jays eager to saddle up and rev the throttle (Figure 4.1).

Making the most of the 'brain gain'

Raj Chaudhuri owns a rather old Ford Fiesta, but it sits gathering dust in the parking space under his apartment. Five days a week Raj takes a rickshaw to Bandra Station where he elbows his way onto the second-class carriage of the downtown train that will, in less than 30 minutes, deposit him at Churchgate Station, close to the city's Victorian-era law courts and the solid, rain-stained, stone buildings of Ballard Estate. He works as an editor for a travel magazine. He'll arrive, spectacles awry and creased after rubbing shoulders, in the most literal sense, with a carriage full of commuters who jostle for space at each station and hang precariously out of open doors as the train speeds from one stop to the next. Mumbai's suburban railways consist of around 250 trains that carry 7.5 million passengers a day. As one of the most overcrowded transport systems in the world, it is not the most comfortable way to travel. There is currently a lone air-conditioned train on one of three lines that run north/south on the peninsula and out to far-flung towns and villages from whence those millions travel everyday into the metropolis for work. Reports in January 2018 suggested that World Bank money might be on its way to make the local train service fully air-conditioned. By the time the new rolling stock's in place it'll be Raj's as yet unborn offspring who will benefit. The 'Mumbai local', as it's colloquially called, is the fastest route up and down the spinnaker of reclaimed land that marks the modern city.

'It's uncomfortable but fast. I'd rather stand with my face in someone's armpit than spend an hour and a half in a car travelling at an average of 10 km an hour', he tells me. Many of his contemporaries shun the train and add to Mumbai's already overcrowded and poorly kept roads by driving, either a motorbike, their own car, or a hailed ride.

Born in Mumbai as the 1980s came to an end, he lived in the city until he was 12 years old and then moved with his family to Azerbaijan where his father was employed in the oil and gas sector. He's part of a small but growing number of young Indians who have been educated abroad and decided to come back to the country of their birth. The 'brain gain' it's been called; a stark contrast to the 'brain drain' that blighted India in the decades after Independence.

He returned in 2013 with a journalism degree from Rutgers, a couple of years' work experience in the US and three years in Oman. He no longer has family in Mumbai but explains the lure thus: 'The opportunities here are greater than say the Middle East, which is actually a tiny market for media jobs. And the immigration challenges for people from the developing world who want to work overseas are massive and getting worse'. I ask him how he saw the changes in India in the 13 years he was away and receive a characteristically colourful reply:

> Previous generations said 'Fuck it, that's the way it is' and did nothing to change it but rather went off in search of a better life. This generation's saying, 'No. Fuck that, we're going to change it'. I feel the country grew wealthier and with that certain sections grew a conscience. Clearly for some there are greater opportunities to live a good life as compared to previous generations.

Although Indian by nationality he feels his years abroad have given him a changed perspective and that expresses itself in many ways. He has an interesting inside-out perspective and doesn't see India as a permanent home, more a stopping off point on a bigger journey.

> I notice cultural differences with my Indian friends who've grown up here. A lot of Indian millennials still look to their parents for guidance on relationships and they often are not sure that they can make the right decisions when it comes to getting married, for example. 'This is such a big decision I'll defer to my parents who know me very well', they say. I know and have always known that those are decisions that I'll make for myself. This is the way things are done here and many of my peer group are comfortable with that.

So here it's not a generational divide but more about the change of mindset that comes from having lived and worked abroad – and dated outside the country. The fact is that, however the match is made, the age at which young urban Indians are marrying is getting later, as we saw earlier.

He loves the work he gets to do and the work culture, which he compares favourably to that he experienced in the Middle East.

> There's more regular meetings and talk about aspects of the business. I feel like I'm learning how to run a media business not just operating in a silo. I'm involved in the commercial aspects and actively working on closer integration between print and digital.
>
> As long as you're learning and you have a constant line of communication open to management and feel appreciated and they give you more and more responsibility, then you feel you're growing. You can't do that if you work in silos and you only know about your tiny bit of the business. If you don't feel like you'll grow into something bigger, you're not going to stay in that job.

He gives the lie to the notion of a generation in need of instant gratification:

> When I think about my friends here and in other parts of the world we're fairly similar in our aspirations. We want a good job and to make a career rather than just earn money. I believe that if you get really good at what you do then the money will follow.

The retreat from public spaces is a feature of modern Indian life earlier noted. For the time being Raj has resisted and continues to take his place at the platform edge and put up with the discomfort of the commute, and an Indian salary much below what he could command elsewhere, because he feels like he's growing professionally and contributing to an era of new growth. His willingness to embrace the city with such gusto, without cynicism, and the realisation that building true value takes time, flies in the face of conventional 'wisdom' on millennial attitudes.

Searching in vain for the *avant garde*

The Beatles famously visited India at the peak of their success. Fifty years on the British government still falls back on the mop tops' ganja-fest in Rishikesh to illustrate the relationship between the two countries. The significance is lost on young Indians whose musical tastes are much more contemporary and more influenced by music emanating from the US.

Until recently not many contemporary chart-topping western musicians performed in the country. A few artists, perhaps in the autumn of their careers, would swing through as part of an Asian leg of a world tour, but *bona fide* international hit makers were few and far between. That is changing slowly as promoters and record companies realise the potential of urban Midnight's Grandchildren as a target audience, willing and able to spend on tickets and merchandise. Improved ease of doing business measures have taken some of the pain out of the minefield of event regulations and the corruption around the acquisition of licences. Festivals such as NH7, Sunburn, and Sula Fest, held each February at Sula Wines' vineyards in Nashik, Maharashtra, will now have a couple of international artists on their line-ups.

Several big-name concerts have been cancelled at the last minute, when permits and approvals were not forthcoming. Metallica, James Blunt, Take That, and David Guetta have all had to cancel tours at short notice.

Lack of live performances are no impediment to young Indians' knowledge about and consumption of international music. iMusic, Google Play, Vodafone Play, and local streaming services Gaana, Hungama, and Saavn provide cheap access to a world of musical content.

Twenty-six-year-old Norwegian DJ and music producer Kyrre Gørvell-Dahll, known by his stage name Kygo, is a global millennial megastar. His brand of remixed EDM (electronic dance music) party tunes is ubiquitous. He played a sold-out set as part of the Sunburn Arena '3-city tour'. A planned date in Delhi had been cancelled a week earlier due to the city's smog and pollution. Around 10,000 young Mumbaikars paid between Rs2,000 (GBP23) and Rs5,000 (GBP58) to see the man of the moment play a makeshift 'arena' constructed on a piece of unkempt, as yet un-built-upon land at Bandra Kurla Complex (BKC), Mumbai's rapidly emerging Central Business District.

This was young urban India at play and dressed to impress. While in other Asian cities, such as Bangkok, Tokyo, or Seoul, young people at music concerts will be testing the boundaries of fashion, the dress code in Mumbai is a pretty standard urban casual – retro-style Adidas Stan Smiths and branded T-shirts in muted tones abound. There's not much individuality and no sense of *avant garde*. The crowd is tribal in its uniformity.

In the dark, with hallucinogenic lasers raking the audience and several thousand smartphones held aloft, we could have been in Vancouver, Milton Keynes, or Chengdu. There remains something intrinsically Indian about large groups of people holding up lights, or *diyas*, supplicant arms raised to a 'holy man' on a stage. The vibe was friendly: less boozy than you'd expect in the west, though Kingfisher beer and Vodka Red Bull were on sale for those willing to miss large parts of the set to join the crush at the bar.

In a culture where close contact and public displays of affection are frowned upon (to the extent of inviting arrest in some instances) and young men and women's occasions to flirt and fornicate are very limited, a concert like this is a rare place of abandon. For many the opportunity was grasped, literally, with both hands.

Respecting tradition, kicking over orthodoxy

The wedding of Kanchi Pandya and Parth Bhatt was unconventional. Most Indian weddings are an opportunity to invite all and sundry. Here only 11 guests, all family members, joined the young couple who had created their own ceremony. Instead of the usual *pandit* (priest) recruited to conduct the ceremony in ancient Sanskrit, a poet presided. 'We wanted it in Gujarati so we understood what vows we were agreeing to. We made the ceremony as simple as possible. It was over in four and a half minutes', the bride says gleefully. The disregard for tradition – no invites were printed, no big party – had collateral consequences. The lack of physical evidence gave the Registrar of Marriages grounds for suspicion. Because he was dubious, he had witnesses sign affidavits to confirm the legitimacy of the marriage.

Few women in India have this level of control over their wedding. Many don't get to choose their own husband, and some may meet him for the first time as the wedding ceremony takes place. To decide whom not to invite to the service is a rare luxury. In another break with orthodoxy Kanchi calls her parents – Chintan and Alka – by their first names. She did so at her parents' behest but had to answer to the headmistress at school who felt it inappropriate and disrespectful. Unabashed, she now follows the same protocol with her in-laws.

If you imagine this is the world of a precocious member of the metro-born elite, you'd be wrong. Kanchi was born in the sprawling port city of Bhavnagar in Gujarat. The city's main claim to fame is that the young Mohandas Gandhi studied at the Alfred High School. She was taught in Gujarati medium. Despite top grades in science subjects her choice was to study Mass Communication and English Literature. Courses included photography, creative writing, and journalism. She decided to become a filmmaker. As a child she says she adored the glamour of what she saw on TV. 'I loved Bollywood. Soaked up interviews with movie stars. Watched endless MTV, Zoom, Zee TV'. She knew no one in an industry that's full of nepotism and tough to crack. She had no insider support. Two of her grandparents and her father were teachers. Her mother's a school administrator.

Her father was very supportive, her mother more cautious:

> I was only 20 when I started working. I had no role model. They hear so many negative stories about the industry. Alka was sceptical. She wanted me to be an academic and publish my papers at a fancy university.

Kanchi persisted. A break came. An advertising agency up from Mumbai hired her as a stagehand. They were making a big budget commercial nearby. None of the crew flown up from the city could speak Gujarati. So she stepped up and got herself a bigger gig. Then she got called back on a larger production. Her brief included scouting, research, workshops, and costume. She assisted the director. Mumbai agencies called her to work on TV commercials. Slowly she built a portfolio and a network and began to do her own projects. She learned the techniques from props assistant to runner and fixer, to assistant director and then principal.

No longer is it the glamour of film and television that appeals. Now it's the process she says that captures her interest. And the format that excites her is documentary. She and her contemporaries are exploring alternative subject areas. The current trend in Indian cinema is towards biopics and other real-life stories. *Pad Man*, the true story of an inventor who makes sanitary products for women in rural India, starring one of Bollywood's biggest heartthrobs, was a surprise hit of early 2018. The millennial quest for authenticity is radically changing the type of content consumed.

In 2013, aged 24, Kanchi made her directorial debut. Some of her work is in English, some in Gujarati. There's a wealth of local-language content being made at present. The arrival of digital technology has spurred that by bringing down production costs dramatically. 'Gujarati films are in vogue and people are making a lot of money there. But whatever it is you have to have a drive to succeed'.

Along the way she met Swaroop Sampat, a former Miss India and now drama and education teacher, who mentored her. With support she carved out a niche for herself. Now she says, 'I'm part of a network, like a circle of support. It goes across generations and it gives you links and connections. Now I'm able to provide some support to the next generation that's coming through'. The movie business is tough, physically and mentally. She hasn't experienced harassment on set 'either by luck or my aura', she adds. She's understood and bought into that very un-millennial notion that professional success takes time and commitment. Gratification will not be instant.

The duality of respect for tradition, and willingness to do it her way, is evident in both professional and personal life. Her knowledge of Indian filmmaking and its protagonists is comprehensive. Some she's had the chance to work with and learn from. She reveres the back catalogue but wants to push boundaries. Her next project is in a genre called 'mumblecore' – I had to look it up! Her wedding was unorthodox, simple, and thoughtful. The needs of all 'concerned persons' were met in the planning and execution. 'I even set up the wedding photographers' cameras so I knew what shots I was getting', she says in parting.

Her infectious blend of tradition and modernity neither offends nor defers. Equally comfortable in sari or sweatpants, she's deeply respectful of her heritage yet writing scripts, for her own life and for her movie productions, overflowing with confidence and subtly challenging conventional attitudes.

On the treadmill in Pune

The Maharastrian city of Pune, another swarming two-wheeler, Tier 2 city, draws students from across western India to its well-respected colleges and universities. Many stay to work in the city's outsourcing companies and tech start-ups, spending their salaries in bars and restaurants and glitzy shopping malls. It's a low-rise city, for now, but becoming rapidly congested as more and more people afford personal mobility. Head south on National Highway 48 and inner city affluence gives way to crumbling outskirts and the farmlands of the Deccan Plain.

Pawan Jani is a Pune boy, part of a new breed of entrepreneur for whom the new India offers a wealth of previously untapped potential. For this 27 year old, born late in 1991, just months after the initiation of economic reforms, the business opportunities are in fitness.

India is not known as a health-conscious nation. In a country experiencing scarcity and high rates of poverty, a sizeable girth was traditionally a visible and tangible sign of affluence for those who could afford it. Rates of lifestyle disease – such as heart disease, high blood pressure, obesity, diabetes – are on the rise. Sixty-one per cent of deaths are due to lifestyle and non-communicable diseases, according to a 2017 report (Down to Earth, 2017),[2] and they affect Indians at younger ages.

For some Indians, particularly young ones in urban areas, health and wellness are becoming more important. Food choices are changing and much more is available in terms of 'low-calorie' substitutes and healthier options than a decade ago. And there's a boom in sports activity, as the popularity of marathons across the country, the proliferation of running clubs and races, and investments by sports brands show. According to Morgan Stanley, more than one-third of Indian millennials have a fitness app installed on their mobile phone (*The Economic Times* 2018).[3]

Sat on a swing outside his gym in Pune's leafy Koregaon Park district, Pawan speaks with confidence and composure. For him fitness is both a lifestyle and a business. He opened his Cross Fit franchise, the first in Pune, in 2014. 'I wasn't a good student in terms of academic performance but I loved sports', he says as the rain teems down on a late-monsoon Friday morning and his core team of fitness trainers bustle around, straightening out equipment as the morning rush subsides. 'Fortunately my parents accepted that and encouraged me. I began working while at college as a fitness instructor. I felt there was an opportunity to do something more community based, where fitness becomes part of a wider lifestyle'.

Traditionally sporting prowess in India has been secondary to academic performance. This is one reason why India has not produced world-class athletes relative to its population. At some stage most promising youngsters succumb to pressure to focus on their academic studies, at the expense of their sporting potential, since that has been seen as a more likely route to career success, stability, and the social acceptance that comes with it. India picked up a silver and a bronze in the 2016 Olympics. China, the only country with a comparable population, took home 70 medals in total. There are exceptions – cricket and hockey are sports in which India has excelled, but in general, whether because of cultural bias or lack of infrastructure and funding, Indian athletes have received little support. 'I was fortunate that my parents took a positive view and were very supportive', says Pawan.

'Fitness is big in India right now', he tells me. Gym membership is on the increase. In July 2017 *The Hindu* reported on the healthy share price of Talwalkers, an 84-year-old Indian fitness group (*The Hindu Business Line*, 2017).[4] Sports equipment and clothing companies are investing heavily. With a few years' experience under their belts, Pawan and his business partner, Akshay Kothavali, see this growth as an opportunity. They've branched out and are now consulting to other gym owners and building a train-the-trainers revenue stream.

He says the clichéd view of millennials wanting immediate gratification, unwilling to put in the hard miles to achieve their potential, is prevalent in the fitness world. The motivation for many at the outset is to get an Instagram-worthy six-pack. Plenty are keen on shortcuts and willing to use steroids and supplements to achieve their objectives. Part of his mission is to change that attitude and to instil the understanding that sustainable performance requires a more dedicated approach. Akshay left IT to move into fitness. That offers a nice vignette of how in a generation a change has taken hold. For the past 20 years IT jobs have held great appeal. Now a growing confidence is inspiring young people like Pawan and Akshay to look at alternative career options to meet growing demand, here for example in wellness and fitness.

Their expansion plans include the launch of a new corporate model in mid-2018. Rather than selling memberships and pulling people into 'the box', as is the model of most commercial gyms, they plan to take their service to corporate campuses, of which Pune has many, with a programme that teaches people to be fit.

> So many people in the IT world lead such sedentary lifestyles sat at a screen for 10 hours a day they end up with back and neck problems in their 30s. We'll run short courses in the office that use a build-measure-learn,

lean-style methodology. There's no shortage of potential customers. It's a local problem and we see a great opportunity to solve that with a completely new business model.

Local in India certainly doesn't mean small. Pune's IT sector employs hundreds of thousands of people and the city is also a centre for the automotive sector and a breeding ground for start-ups. Pawan will have no shortage of sedentary desk-jockeys to work with over the coming decade. Changing attitudes to lifestyle, driven by better education and rising levels of disposable income, are creating new market segments and willing consumers.

Into India's farming heartlands

The sleeper train for Nagpur departs as the sun sets over Mumbai's Chhatrapati Shivaji Maharaj Terminus, a Raj-era Gothic Revival edifice, formerly named Victoria Terminus and colloquially still known as 'VT'. The platform is long and cluttered with travellers, baggage, and trollies piled high with string-tied boxes to be dispatched to far-flung corners of the country. Passenger names (with ages prominently displayed) are neatly printed on the manifest pasted to the side of the train. In two-tier 2nd class AC (air-conditioned) compartments the padded bench forms one bed and the backrest pulls up to create the upper bunk. Crisp, white, freshly ironed sheets are delivered in brown paper wrapping and as the coaches head eastward, sprightly boys jump on board at every stop to serve hot chai and samosas. Around 5 am the pale morning light seeps into the sky over eastern Maharashtra as the train trundles through

Figure 4.2

millions of acres of farmland towards its destination in the centre of India. Physically and culturally this is a long way from the urban clutter of Mumbai.

Kartikeya Tutwala, my nephew, was a toddler when I first came to India and is now a young man finding his place in the world. He greeted me warmly at Dhamangaon Station and walked me through the narrow streets of the old town to the second-storey room he rents from the headmaster of a local school. Born in 1994 and brought up in Mumbai's western suburbs he gained a degree in Ancient Indian Culture at St. Xavier's College in Mumbai in 2015 and then, to the bemusement of his parents, decided to study agriculture. He has a notion to develop a business focused on a return to traditional methods of crop rotation and a field-to-fork supply chain. Bag packed he headed into the hinterlands and spent a year living in a farming community to conduct an experiment and understand the rhythms of rural life. 'The problems faced by farmers are not new and they're on a huge scale. So it's scary and exciting to think about how you might contribute', he says.

This kind of bold, adventurous spirit is to be encouraged, so I decided to visit for a couple of days. I wanted to get a flavour of the place Kartikeya had chosen. I was intrigued to think about how the life chances and aspirations of his fellow millennials in rural India compared or contrasted with those of his urban classmates and the impact that mass urbanisation has on rural communities and those who don't leave. He told me:

> Rural and urban India are interdependent but developing in parallel rather than in unison. People in cities and villages don't know what's happening in the other place. Most of the farmers I'm working with are the same age as my father. The younger people are moving to the cities. Very few want to work the land. It's a problem. Farming, as its been practised for generations, offers no economic stability.

He knows he's been privileged to have the chance to study something arcane rather than have to acquire practical skills that more directly support a family, as is the case for young men in farming communities. 'If you're born in rural India you don't have that luxury', he says.

Prashant Dagwar is one such young man. A 28-year-old farmer, he and Kartikeya have worked together on a pilot project to compare farming methods and measure the success of alternative pesticides. Prashant's mother tongue is Marathi and Kartikeya acts as our translator. He's a third-generation farmer, Prashant tells me:

> My great grandfather sold locally brewed alcohol. Because of the ill will that comes with that occupation, my grandfather left the business and started farming. Since then we've been occupational farmers. My

grandfather owned four acres of land and we eventually bought two more acres over a period of time. So, our family holding is six acres today. In order to feed all the ten mouths in our family and earn more we rent another ten acres of land.

The joint family consists of two brothers, two sisters-in-law, their three children, and his parents. Prashant would like to get married but his perceived lowly status as a farmer isn't helping.

It's so difficult for a young farmer to get married. None of the villagers want to marry their daughters to a farmer. They all want and aspire to a person who has a government job or is a businessman or a city dweller. Nobody wants to build ties with us. A farmer's son does not want to be a farmer.

Only one of the brothers is a full-time farmer; they're trying to diversify and protect themselves from the desperation that a failed crop brings. One brother now drives an auto-rickshaw and Prashant is studying a BSc in Agriculture from the Open University with a view to opening an alternative route for himself. He works part time for an NGO that supports farmers too. He says he has no desire to move to the city. 'Even if I get far less money than I wish to earn, I would rather stay in my village than else-where. I am really happy'.

For many the lure of urban life is powerful and an opportunity to escape the harsh realities of farming. Many reasons are put forward to explain the persistently high suicide rates in these communities. The current govern-ment's objective of doubling farmers' incomes by 2022 may have an impact but the situation is more complex than just financial. Social structures for Prashant remain highly traditional as his observations on his marriage prospects suggest. Spending is tightly controlled: 'We spend money at Diwali', he tells me.

The next morning we eat breakfast – spicy *poha*, a traditional Mahar-ashtrian dish of flattened rice with onions, peanuts, and curry leaves – and drink sweet tea in a neat little family-run café whose owner has taken my nephew under his wing. My status as Kartikeya's uncle causes much debate and a level of disbelief that doesn't exist in my usual urban setting where a mixed marriage is unusual but not outside the realms of experience. Here its newsworthiness means I'm interviewed for the local TV channel. Kartikeya reflects on some of the things he's learned. The pervasive influence of caste in this community has surprised him.

I've grown up in a place where caste isn't a topic. Mumbai is very mixed. In the community we're in now it's a fundamental factor. Inter-caste marriages [are a] cause of much social stigma. They're seen as a problem, a blot to be erased.

He's known couples who've had to abscond because they've dated across caste boundaries and returning home would be dangerous, possibly life threatening. And caste plays a part in many other aspects of life.

> As an outsider it's difficult to understand the complexities but I've seen that caste plays an important role in this community and who will work with who and how they manage their relationships. It's easy to find yourself caught in the middle of that.

Kartikeya clearly feels himself a beneficiary of the opportunity that modern India presents. He's grown up in relative affluence and can afford to break with tradition rather than following the footsteps of his father who followed his father into the family steel-trading business. Do his small-town contemporaries share that optimism?

> We all have the same access to information, so our knowledge of the world may be common. Prashant and others tell me they're optimistic, but the realities of their lives are so different from mine that the comparison doesn't really have meaning. It's difficult to see farming as a realistic livelihood for future generations. So the problem is that those that can leave and head to the cities, and that weakens these communities.

India's urbanisation is one of its great appeals. Its cities are the powerhouses of its economic growth and beacons of hope and opportunity for young people. But the families and communities they leave behind are less sustainable and more marginalised as young people turn their backs on rural life. As dusk settles on Dhamangaon Station I board the evening train back to Mumbai. I'm inspired by Kartikeya's investment of time to understand the dynamic of urbanisation and the tensions of tradition and modernity and his willingness to expend energy looking in the opposite direction rather than just exploiting the privilege he was born to.

Traffic is not all one way

'Keralans eat a lot of fish but not usually so raw'. Stacy Samuels was reliving her foreign exchange trip to Copenhagen with the confidence that comes from plenty of international travel, and a palate for good food. Unlike Raj Chaudhuri, born in Mumbai and returning to a place he knew, Stacy has a different migration story.

She's been at her job as a copywriter with advertising agency Rickshaw for four weeks.

She describes herself as third-generation NRI – a 'non-resident Indian', a term used loosely to cover Indians living abroad and others with Indian heritage. Her parents, like many Indians from the fish-loving coastal state of Kerala, are in Dubai and her grandparents previously in Malaysia – another great fish-favouring cuisine! The Middle East still holds appeal for many young Indians. The reality when they manage to get visas and residency often doesn't match the pictures in the brochure. For Stacy the pull of India was strong.

> I made the choice to come back. I moved to Abu Dhabi when I was four. I've seen my father run a business in the UAE that contributes to the UAE economy, not ours. And it's easy for us to sit either there or in India and complain about things in India; poverty, slums, lack of education. You can blame the government but it's another thing to come here and be in it, and do something about it and try to make a change. So I want to do something for my country, not someone else's country and I primarily identify as Indian. I want to make sure everything I do is for this country and its growth.

She says that the fact that there are more opportunities now in India was of secondary concern. Brimming with optimism she tells me: 'I'm fortunate in that I've never known a world where there weren't these opportunities'.

But she takes issue with my use of the term millennial.

> I am what I am and now I'm seen as part of a generalisation. Each person has something unique to offer. Just because of the age doesn't mean we are all the same. I don't think it's right for you to just say millennials, this and that.

She's not held back by any traditional sense of deference.

By the end of the interview she's turned the tables and is quizzing me on the terror attacks in London and Manchester and why the UK has become a target and whether the terrible fire at Grenfell Tower in Kensington, West London, screened live in India courtesy of BBC World 24 hours before our interview, was a terror event. Her level of knowledge of and interest in foreign affairs is uncommon – even for this cohort that is broadly exposed to foreign media – and wonderfully encouraging. So with qualifications from Pune's prestigious Symbiosis College under her arm, and a hat full of bombast, she's off to change the world. 'And watch Game of Thrones!'

Reinvention in India's tech city

Bangalore, the south Indian city officially known as Bengaluru but still typically called by its traditional name, is India's tech hub, the so-called 'Silicon Valley of India', renowned for its call centres and soul-destroying traffic. Arriving in the city on the Hindu festival of Shivratri, a public holiday on a crisp February morning, the roads were clear and my progress, from the far-flung airport to city centre, unexpectedly unimpeded.

Figure 4.3

Since the mid-1990s Bangalore has boomed as a generation of entrepreneurs began to tap the deep pool of engineering talent emanating from the city's prestigious colleges and universities. This is the birthplace of India's Business Process Outsourcing (BPO) industry. Long shifts at unsociable hours fixing problems for customers in the US or checking data for European banking corporations have funded the dreams of a generation of young aspiring Indians. Jobs aplenty, attrition rates have been high as young people moved for better salaries and bigger designations. It's a fast-moving and dynamic employment market. The city oozes aspiration and affluence. Its broad downtown avenues are lined with high-end stores, fashionable bars, and shared workspaces. Coffee shops on the stylish 80ft Road and its tributaries in Koramangala attract a crowd of tech start-up entrepreneurs. At an average age of just 28.5 years, Bangalore's entrepreneurs are said to be the youngest in the world (*The Times of India*, 2015).[5]

Tech giants Infosys, Wipro, and Mindshare were all founded and head-quartered in Bangalore. Tata Consultancy Services and other large technology businesses are also big employers in the city, bussing huge numbers of staff from outlying residential areas to giant, manicured IT campuses that mimic their Californian counterparts. While these multi-billion dollar businesses grab the headlines, the reality is that most jobs in Bangalore's US$150 billion IT/ITES industry are created by small and medium-size enterprises (SMEs).

Austere Analytics is a three-year-old data analytics business specialising in the healthcare industry. It employs 25 people with an average age of around 30 years. Co-founder Onkar (he uses only one name) is above the median of Bangalorian entrepreneurs – at 35 he scrapes into the millennial cohort. He came to the city in the early 2000s as a student. From a modest background, his father is a government employee and his mother a homemaker, he left his home town, 200 km outside Kolkata in West Bengal, to study biotechnology in Bangalore. He graduated, stayed, and joined the outsourcing industry. With almost a decade in the BPO sector under his belt, including a stint with Genpact, the BPO spun out of GE, he felt it was time to set up on his own. He reinvented himself as a business owner. Bangalore is a place of reinvention. In 30 years it has transformed from a garden city with a population of a mere 3.7 million to a metropolis of more than 10 million. More migrants flood in every week. For many young Indians it holds the promise of economic independence and a chance to throw off the shackles of the past unbounded by the restraints of family, caste, or geography.

Onkar chooses his words with care. Smartly dressed in a no-frills boardroom, he describes the 'thought process' that went into envisioning the business and the 'baby steps' he and his co-founders, Tarun Sinha and Nandini Indiran, took.

> Finding the right people is a challenge. There are lots of highly qualified graduates, but finding the ones with a good balance of technical skills and attitude isn't easy. We're focused on creating an open culture and a heterogeneous environment that enables people to flourish.

He tells me that 70 per cent of Bangalore's population is from elsewhere, so there's a great deal of diversity in the population.

He takes his responsibilities as an employer seriously. He 'walks the talk' by meeting each of his employees for a one-to-one discussion twice a month and works hard to balance what he sees as a need for hierarchy with a milieu within which his team feels empowered.

> I genuinely listen. I give feedback. I've done it since we began the business. At the outset people maybe didn't relate well to that approach but it's become part of our culture. I encourage it down the line so it's not just an individual activity.

In an industry where attrition of 20 per cent and more is the norm he's been able to halve that rate. He describes two groups of employees: one with industry experience, the other 'freshers' whom he can mould.

I met half a dozen of the former group. Enthusiastic, forthright, they've come into the office on a public holiday to meet and share their stories with me. Two Karticks (K and S), Keerthi, Nivsakar, Sweta, and co-founder Tarun are all internal migrants who've made Bangalore home – at least for now. The first four are all from the neighbouring state of Tamil Nadu, Sweta and Tarun from north India. At least three have worked for much bigger tech companies such as Tata Consultancy Services, Genpact, and Empower, behemoths that employ tens of thousands of people. Each joined Austere because they wanted a place where they wouldn't get lost in the crowd. 'A small team means you have direct access to the leadership and that's really important', says Kartick S. He and Onkar are the only unmarried members of the group. He's enjoying dating in a city where there are plenty of bars and places to meet girls and a freedom that's not available to him back home under the watchful eyes of kith and kin. Kartick is optimistic about his chances of finding a partner without recourse to an arranged marriage. Nivsakar, married (arranged) and with a young child, expects to return to Chennai soon because he wants his child to be educated in Tamil and in a system he knows and trusts. His reinvention is partial.

With money to spend they're all enjoying the lifestyle that well-paid jobs in Bangalore open up. They have a fondness for international brands and a willingness to spend rather than save.

Internal migration, from which Bangalore benefits massively, means the city has a vibrant mix of cultures. Festivals of all hues and histories are celebrated, movies play in multiple languages, and there's no shortage of food from every corner of India available within a short cab ride.

But there's a dark side too. All are mindful that not everyone welcomes the out-of-towners drawn by the lure of jobs. Bangalore's rapid emergence and the gentrification that's accompanied it in the past decades hasn't benefitted all equally. 'There's a real undercurrent of sentiment that people from outside have come and taken jobs and pushed up prices. Whether that's envy or jealousy you feel it', Onkar says.

Bangalore is a metaphor for contemporary India: growing fast, reinventing itself, more meritocratic than past incarnations, buzzing with optimism yet failing to get to grips with the inequality that development brings with it. Fun and frustrating in equal measure.

Setting sail for international experience

Viren Arora spoke to me the day before he left Delhi for Berlin to start a new job. Twenty-four years old, he's already raised funds for, launched, and wound up one start-up. His first venture, MyButler, was a short-lived food delivery service focused on a high-end clientele primarily in New Delhi's prosperous southern enclaves, the natural habitat of wealthy, Indian, baby-boomer, and Gen X professionals and foreign expatriates for whom a Rs2,500 (GBP30) ticket price for food delivered from one of the kitchens in the Oberoi Hotel or Olive Bar & Grill is small change.

Over coffee he confesses that his pitch deck was built during three months at the desk he'd been given in his first job having left Mumbai University with a degree in Business Administration. The job, with an established B2B real estate business, was a decent entry-level role with a monthly salary of Rs40,000 (GBP450). Within two weeks he'd had an allergic reaction.

> Culturally it was abhorrent to me. The focus was on decorum not delivery. The practices and processes were trite. Management was

uninspiring. There was no visible reliance on or application of technology. I couldn't envisage myself growing in that environment.

So he took the leap and became an entrepreneur – with family support, both moral and financial. He was, he says on reflection, naïve and arrogant about his ability to raise capital. He turned down an early offer of INR5 million (US$77,500) because it required him to give 25 per cent equity and he thought he'd get a better deal. When he did need a cash injection he couldn't find willing bidders and took the call that he'd be better off getting some more experience. He says he'll set something up in the future. Job offers from Indian tech start-ups were declined because he felt he'd benefit from some international experience.

He sees that deferring his entrepreneurial journey may well in the long run deliver greater value. It goes against the received wisdom of millennials as entitled and unwilling to wait. He is able to frame his 'failure' with MyButler as a vital and enriching experience, 'a learning'. He clearly learned a lot – about himself as well as the world of business – and can see how that adds to his credentials.

Does he think a prospective father- or mother-in-law might see his patchy résumé negatively? He laughs: 'Never have I seen any of my decisions through that lens. I've never even thought about whether that would jeopardise my marriage prospects'. The age at which pressure to marry is exerted is getting later but it's still very real, he says: 'That's particularly true for women. Large numbers of well-educated young women are still not able to make their contribution and participate in the workforce. There's parental pressure for them to marry and become homemakers'.

Past generations did not have the luxury to take such a pragmatic view of a 'false start'. His story signals a changing cultural context where the old markers of professional progressions, status, value of time served, and continuity are being replaced by other measures. Pressure to conform, professionally and socially, has not disappeared, but more leeway is being extended.

Returning and reimagining

The Leela is one of Mumbai's many luxury hotels. Liveried doormen nod courteously and greet guests with a prayerful salute: 'Namaste'. The marble-floored foyer is spotless and airy. Corridors of thick pile carpet lead to sumptuous, artfully designed rooms. Wedding groups mingle and businessmen and women strike deals on the deep sofas of the coffee lounge. It's an oasis of calm a mile from the international airport and the thundering traffic of Andheri-Kurla Road, currently more congested than usual as the digging to lay the foundations of Mumbai's much needed metro disrupts. The Leela was a pioneer of India's five star service culture. Its founder was the opulently named Captain Chittarath Poovakkatt ('CP') Krishnan Nair a former Indian army officer turned industrialist. A few years after Indian

Figure 4.4

Independence, as a young man in the 1950s he founded a fabrics business. In his mid-sixties, influenced by the plush hotels he'd experienced on business trips to Europe, he envisaged a chain of luxury hotels in India and embarked on a third career as an hotelier. Named after his wife, the hotel opened in the late 1980s.

Amruda Nair is his millennial granddaughter and a hospitality entrepreneur in her own right. She grew up in the hotel and spent time in the family business before branching out on her own and launching the Aiana brand of hotels. She's aware of her privileged status.

Captain Nair's military discipline is apparent in the precision with which the hotel functions. His granddaughter has inherited that ethic. It is evident in her disciplined approach to work and presentation. She's precise in her thinking, articulate, speedy in her delivery, and impeccably attired.

Over coffee she tells me:

> I think the biggest difference from my parents' generation has been the desire to come back and participate in the growth story. In the past if you could afford to go abroad for education then you stayed there and made a life for yourself. That was what families talked about and you saw it in the matrimonial adverts in newspapers. That was the aspiration.

Educated in London, Amsterdam, New York, and Singapore there's no sense in which her international education is being wasted. And given her already exalted social standing, the university degrees are no mere bargaining chips to push up her marriage chances. She's worked across Asia and held roles across functions. Coming back to India was always her intention – but not only to work in an established family business.

She says:

> In my case everyone wanted to go and study abroad and then maybe stay for a year or two to get experience and work with the right brands, but the intent was always there to come back. That's where the shift happened. After 2000 a lot changed and suddenly India was the place to be. The professional opportunities were in India.

Competition for roles was tough, even for the scion of an established and successful family, and her international experience helped differentiate her. From 2008 she spent seven years in the family business, a period in which the Leela Group expanded rapidly under her father's stewardship.

She'd contributed to the growth, applying the skills and processes in asset management she'd learned outside to the established family business. She'd proved her worth but felt a strong urge to do something on her own.

> The fact that I'd worked with other brands and big companies made a difference to the way I was seen and accepted. I think you need to be accepted and people need to value you for who you are. But my desire to be recognised as an individual was stronger than my desire to assimilate. I didn't want to be plugged into the existing system.

The Leela Palaces – the group has other properties in Goa, Bangalore, Chennai, New Delhi, Udaipur, and Kovalam – offer quintessential traditional Indian luxury hospitality. But they lack appeal to a new generation of travellers, uninterested in pomp and circumstance and in search of something less formal. In 2015, a year after her grandfather's death, Amruda launched Aiana with backing from a Middle Eastern investor. Aiana is meeting the needs of a new breed of experience-hungry travellers with a form of what she describes as 'affordable luxury'.

Amruda is part of a growing number of young Indians who could have made successful careers for themselves outside India. Instead they're choosing to pack their bags and come back, well qualified, ambitious, and confident that they can achieve things in India. They bring with them new ideas, and a discipline that's too often been lacking in even their seemingly well-run family businesses. Their desire to succeed, in some cases to reinvent themselves, to use their creative and entrepreneurial talents to create value in India, is exciting.

When talent management fails

Not all Midnight's Grandchildren live in India. The numbers of non-resident Indians or people of Indian origin who reside in other countries are huge. The Indian government puts the number of such people at around 20 million (Non Resident Indian Online, 1997).[6] The United Nations Department of Economic and Social Affairs is more cautious but still puts the sum at around 16 million (*The Times of India*, 2016),[7] which still ranks it the largest diaspora on the planet. Through these migrants many people across the planet have an arms-length but deep affinity with the country. Overseas Indians contribute significantly to the country's finances. Inbound remittances to India from the diaspora were around US$65 billion in 2017, according to the World Bank (*The Economic Times*, 2017),[8] the highest received by any country, and more than 4 per cent of total GDP.

The diaspora is an important source of soft power for India. Indians abroad give the rest of the world a perspective on the country. By transporting and maintaining their traditions, culture, and values across generations they are vital ambassadors.

The number of Indian-origin millennials with great desire to leave the surroundings in which they've grown up to move back to India may be small. Most somewhat begrudgingly make occasional trips to visit aged relatives in far-flung corners of the country.

Sureka Rao is an exception. A global Indian by any measure she was born in the US, and went to school there and in Switzerland, Thailand, and India. She adjusted to a period of time in junior school in Vadodara in Gujarat and then had a couple of years as a boarder in one of Bangalore's plethora of international schools. She grew up in a home where her mother spoke English and her father, the south Indian language Telugu.

In 2010 she came to work in India for a market research company that seconded her from the US as part of its emerging leaders programme. She felt at home and what she describes as a 'real sense of belonging'. But the contrasts in working styles in India and the US were stark. In the US she'd worked under enlightened managers who saw her potential, coached her, and supported her with stretch projects and development plans. In India she came up against poor leadership in a culture she says lacked transparency that allowed 'shady practices' to go unchallenged.

> There were lots of cultural differences to be accommodated. I was accustomed to be in constant contact with leaders. I was on first name terms with them and had the confidence to push back and challenge. There was a lot of mentoring and career planning alongside the functional tasks. In India I found myself with a boss who was what I'd describe as 'a typical Delhi guy' – loved playing politics, very keen to have people around him to make him look good, not interested in my career development, not good at giving feedback and very ad hoc.

While at a national level within the firm there was, she says, a desire to professionalise the Indian arm of the business, those efforts were undermined down the line in an unreformed culture of opacity and unethical behaviours.

She quit. She co-founded an events business. Even in that role, working with a former school friend who'd grown up in India, she struggled to deal with the cultural differences. 'In terms of skill sets we were well matched and complemented each other but there were lots of clashes about working styles. There were double standards that I couldn't handle'.

Her pockets full of lessons from her foray into entrepreneurship, she moved to London and completed a Masters' degree from the London Business School. In late 2017 she began work in the UK for a global financial services organisation and has the world at her feet. Yet she still feels a solid pull to India and wants at some point to return. 'My US passport helps me travel but I feel strongly Indian', she says.

Indian companies need to think hard about their engagement strategies if they are to attract eloquent and ambitious leaders-in-waiting with familial links and powerful urges to participate in the country's growth. If they're part of international groups they must make sure there's consistency across regions – not to homogenise and eradicate the local flavour but to build cultures that will enable young talent to flourish, not flee.

Key takeaways

1 **Brimming with confidence.** This group is not short on confidence and optimism about the future. They have it in spades. This sample hasn't known anything but a world of opportunity and sees its destiny as a new book waiting to be written rather than a postscript or update to a previous one scripted by its forefathers. The optimism is not misplaced. The confidence is not always warranted and sometimes hides a lack of self-awareness and inability to step into the shoes of others and see the world from their perspectives. Nevertheless it is infectious.

2 **Millennialism as an evolving mindset.** The Indian millennial mindset shares some common traits with its western counterpart, but has inimitably Indian characteristics. The ties that bind to tradition are still in many instances stronger than is the case in more developed nations where 'freedom' and 'autonomy' are more established. The desire for independence is still, for many, secondary to a desire to belong. This is a transitional phase where two sets of ideologies have to coexist. For now there is a gap between the expressed attitudes, and the degree to which they can be lived out. Ties to more traditional values and behaviours will continue to weaken over time as the attitudes become more established and as this group takes centre stage as the majority of the working population, wage earners, and consumers. The mindset will become more firmly entrenched

and hegemonic as its proponents assert their authority. It will remain pervasive as the next generation of young people – Gen Z, those currently under 18 – come of age and continue the nation's modernising drive.

3   **Still willing to put in the hard miles.** Desire for instant gratification hasn't completely taken over. Many of these young people clearly understand the need to put in the effort to build their own value over time. They subscribe to what in the west would be described as 'middle-class values' – a strong work ethic and understanding that job success comes neither easily nor quickly. They welcome and look for supportive environments where they see long-term potential to co-create value. Their optimism about the future means they'll jump ship quickly if that need is not met.

4   **The desire to contribute is powerful.** A formidable desire exists to contribute to the country's next phase of growth rather than succumb to the earlier generations' desire to migrate and build lives elsewhere. International exposure is valued and seen as desirable but as a stepping stone to contributing and creating value in India. Rapid growth and advances in technology are creating previously unidentified or non-existent opportunities. Even young people of Indian origin born and raised in developed nations see opportunity and excitement in the world's fastest growing large economy and feel a strong pull.

5   **Migration creates momentum.** Internal migration is a powerful source of energy and a driver of change. It allows people to develop identities, ideas, and careers away from the ties that bind when they live closer to family and tradition. Some reinvent themselves by transporting with them a set of values and traditions and reinterpreting them in a new milieu. My experience as an employer is that recruits who've fled the nest and moved within the country are better qualified to succeed (whatever technical skills they have, or lack) and more likely to acquire self-awareness and be engaged. But the communities they leave behind are weakened and less sustainable as a result.

Notes

1 *The Times of India*, 2017. India is now the world's biggest two-wheeler market. Available at https://timesofindia.indiatimes.com/auto/bikes/india-is-now-worlds-biggest-2-wheeler-market/articleshow/58555735.cms. Accessed on 23/07/2018.

2 Down to Earth, 2017. Lifestyle diseases are the biggest killers in India. Available at www.downtoearth.org.in/news/lifestyle-diseases-are-the-biggest-killer-in-india-59235. Accessed on 23/07/2018.

3 *The Economic Times*, 2018. https://economictimes.indiatimes.com/wealth/plan/are-millennials-financially-wiser-than-their-parents-find-out/articleshow/65268296.cms. Accessed on 28/09/2018.

4 *The Hindu Business Line*, 2017. Talwalkars' shares to see healthy rise. Available at www.thehindubusinessline.com/markets/stock-markets/talwalkars-shares-to-see-healthy-rise/article9760602.ece. Accessed on 23/07/2018.

5 *The Times of India*, 2015. At average 28.5 yrs, Bengaluru has youngest entrepreneurs in world. Available at https://timesofindia.indiatimes.com/business/india-business/At-average-28-5-yrs-Bengaluru-has-youngest-entrepreneurs-in-world/arti cleshow/48259945.cms#. Accessed on 23/07/2018.

6 Non Resident Indian Online, 1997. Statistics of Indians abroad. Available at www.nriol.com/indiandiaspora/statistics-indians-abroad.asp. Accessed on 23/07/ 2018.

7 *The Times of India*, 2016. India has largest diaspora population in world, UN report says. Available at https://timesofindia.indiatimes.com/nri/other-news/India-has-largest-diaspora-population-in-world-UN-report-says/articleshow/50572695. cms. Accessed on 23/07/2018.

8 *The Economic Times*, 2017. India to be the top recipient of remittances from its diaspora in 2017. Available at https://economictimes.indiatimes.com/nri/forex-and-remittance/india-to-be-the-top-recipient-of-remittances-from-its-diaspora-in-2017/articleshow/60926915.cms. Accessed on 23/07/2018.

5   Millennials in the workplace

Pecking orders are powerful

The headline on the front page of India's pink paper *The Economic Times* caught my eye: 'Tata Motors Scraps Designations to Create a Flatter Organisation, Boost Creativity' (*The Economic Times*, 2017).[1] Beneath this headline lay an important story that sets the context for a discussion of India's workplaces and the forces at play in this moment of change. Like all the best stories it has a twist in its tail.

The story reported how Tata Motors – the automotive arm of the sprawling Tata group – had scrapped a range of titles including those of general manager, senior general manager, deputy general manager, vice-president, and senior vice-president among others. This change reduced the number of supervisory ranks from 14 to five. The move affected around 10,000 employees. The report quoted the company, saying it was designed to create a 'mind set free of designations and hierarchy' and help Tata Motors put in place a work culture that's in line with those at global companies especially service organisations. Time-bound promotions would end and only occur when vacancies were to be filled. The newspaper said it had learnt that 'the response to the move has been mixed, with younger employees reacting with greater enthusiasm than those older'.

Six weeks after it announced its bold, reformist, delayering move Tata Motors said it had reversed its decision. Recently redundant designations were reinstated. A company spokesperson was quoted saying: 'Cultural change is a journey and we will keep our pace with it. Our employees' voice and their engagement is the most important topic under our action agenda currently and hence this decision'.

The Hindu's online channel Businessline.com (2017) commented:

> In the Indian context, hierarchy is a big thing even though it may not be such a big deal in the West. Even while the Tata Motors' initiative made news across industry circles, there were enough people who were not completely convinced that it would work. It is now crystal clear that the company has decided not to rock the boat. It is quite likely that

employees were concerned about external perception and how other associates in the supply chain, such as dealers and suppliers, would gauge their standing in the new 'designation-less' regime.[2]

Titles are more than mere symbols. Designations are important markers of success and social standing. Wholesale reform of job titles seems to have inflamed the traditionalists and mobilised resistance. Modernisers in Indian organisations have a major job on their hands to change traditional work-place culture in which rank and seniority continue to define status and identity.

The story (which I'm sure will have an epilogue, perhaps currently being drafted) illustrates several points useful in understanding the disruptions being caused in the workplace, as millennials become the dominant cohort in the Indian workforce. It tells us that:

- some enlightened Indian corporations are seeking to change their structures, policies and approaches to career management;
- unless companies deal with the thorny issue of culture change, the structural change is unlikely to succeed;
- flatter, less hierarchical structures appeal to younger workers but the cultural context within which young Indians grow means they are ill equipped to function successfully in those environments;
- change is messy and uneven and success is not guaranteed;
- with vested interest in the status quo, resistance from the old order may be fierce and can jeopardise progress;
- external perceptions are core to many Indian's feeling of self-worth.

The last point provides important context for understanding the story. A sense of relativity, my value in relation to that of others', is deep rooted in India. It's not surprising given the highly stratified nature of Indian society and its legacy of caste. But there's more to it.

I note how many Indians remain in regular contact with their 'batch mates', the contemporaries who graduated in the same year. This is more in evidence in India than in any other country in which I've lived and worked. It has been abetted by the arrival of professional networking platforms in the past 10–15 years that let us stalk our former colleagues at will. Professional Indian men (men in particular) have a detailed knowledge of what each of their batch mates is doing. What they're earning. To whom they report. Where each sits in a complex web of stratification. Even those who have departed for pastures new abroad are not immune. The relativity of their professional and social success is tracked, and traded.

Amrit Thomas, Diageo's marketing chief, offered me this explanation:

> We grew up with a scarcity mindset and therefore it was highly competitive and you grew up and were celebrated on things like ranks

and what college you got into and chided when you were less successful than others. That culture drove this need to compare as a mark on whether you're progressing.

In an era of scarcity, lack of opportunity, and uncertainty, 'career' offered a realm of stability. It was largely predictable when other areas of life were not. A good job enhanced marriage prospects. Annual increments, rising designations (often accompanied by non-cash bonuses such as household appliances) were a tangible measure of advancement. A paternalistic and highly ordered work culture offered a comfortable security blanket. Performance was not the key metric. Time served counted for more. Generations of Indians have benefitted moving steadily up the ranks and building social capital as they did so.

Within the workplace, the default 'engagement' model was top-down, command and control. It left little room for individual initiative, discouraged risk taking and stifled creativity. Decision making was highly centralised. Trust was in short supply and remains scare. India's current crop of middle and senior managers – a group with 10 to 30 years' experience – continue to draw succour from those certainties and are reluctant to be robbed of that frame of reference.

But social standing and the signposts of success are changing, Amrit tells me:

> Today those markers are different. We've started to think about how millennials are living their lives. Are they fulfilled? Are they having fun? Are they balanced? Are they making an impact? Is what they're doing connected to a passion? That's the millennial discussion.

A tipping point approaches

Indian workplaces are evidently experiencing a period of transition. Offices and factories are battlegrounds on which the clash of tradition and modernity is being played out. Millennials already make up 46 per cent of the working-age population in India, according to Forbes (2017).[3] They will soon account for the majority of employees. Organisations have to find a balance. They must respond to the increasingly vocal demands of young workers seeking a more dynamic career environment and the expectations of a previous generation who grew up with a scarcity mindset. For them, command and control is still the default setting. Companies need to present an employee value proposition that will appeal to young, ambitious new recruits without pulling the rug from under those who are charged with leading them.

Structural changes such as delayering are part of the answer. More fundamental is the need to change corporate culture in ways that engage broadly, alienating neither group but preparing all for a future that looks very different from the past.

Inside out and outside in

Researching this book I had the privilege to meet several experienced Indian human resources (HR) leaders and business heads. They represent a range of sectors with operations in different parts of the country. With them I discussed the challenges, and importantly opportunities, that the millennial mindset presents. I also interviewed mediators such as recruitment consultants and coaches. They offer an inside-out perspective on the needs and wants of organisations and an outside-in view on the aspirations of job seekers. Some were well known to me and the conversations took place over time as ideas evolved. Others I met once, solely for the purpose of this book. Combined, their experiences and ideas provide an insight into a moment of transformation in the country's workplaces.

I found a like-minded advocate for Hofstede's Cultural Dimensions Theory in P Padmakumar. PK, as he's universally known, has, for the past 30 years, been fleet of foot and unafraid to move frequently between roles. He is something of a proto-millennial despite the specks of grey showing through his neatly combed hair. He has scripted an impressive résumé across several industry verticals handling operations roles as well as HR functions. I met him in Chennai, the capital of the southerly state of Tamil Nadu, at the fag end of the southwest monsoon. The streets still waterlogged, I had to jump gingerly over muddy puddles, side stepping *chai-wallas* and curb-side cows as I made my way to the dry haven of his high-rise office.

PK is currently HR team leader of French multinational Saint Gobain's glass business in India. He met me at 8.30 am, an uncommonly early hour for an Indian executive to take meetings, and we talked for three hours, a generous allocation of time by any busy executive's standards.

Under PK's direction, Saint Gobain has mapped its corporate culture against the accepted Hofstede measures for India. He uses this comparison to show me where India naturally overlaps with the global Saint Gobain culture and the areas where he's made efforts to close the gap. Values, he says, are universal across Saint Gobain. Cultural differences are accommodated and celebrated. 'If you're in Rome, be a Roman. When in India, be Indian!'

This mapping showed the power distance dimension as the one with the lowest level of overlap on the company/country matrix. Saint Gobain has addressed it in several ways. Designation is one. For external consumption Saint Gobain has only two designations: team member and team leader. Despite his own extensive experience, seniority, and multiple responsibilities that cover several of Saint Gobain's Indian businesses, PK sticks with the title 'team leader'. It's a powerful sign of values in action. There are, he acknowledges, internal grades used to manage remuneration. 'But designation is not a social marker. We tell applicants if you're looking for money or status, then Saint Gobain is not the place for you. We don't use titles such as workman, technician, or operator', he says.

Other day-to-day attempts to reduce power distance include provision of uniforms, a common canteen for all staff, and family days at which all employees mingle.

Cynics have told him it'll work in south India – deemed by some as more 'evolved', it has high literacy and low birth rates – but not in north India where status and rank are still highly prized. He says evidence proves otherwise: 'We've acquired businesses in Rajasthan and Gujarat and been able to introduce the "team member", "team leader" format without losing more than one or two people, despite the dire warnings'.

I put it to him that by virtue of being a multinational inbound investor to India it must be easier to introduce and sustain these flatter structures. 'The French are very hierarchical', he shoots back, and I sense that delayering is a battle not only to be fought on the shop floor in India but that it must be won too in the executive suites of corporate headquarters in La Défense.

Despite PK's claim that he's been able to deal with power distance at a pan-India level, there's a case to make that given the country's scale and complexity, some, possibly all, of Hofstede's dimensions warrant more localised analysis. Power distance, for example, may not be so extreme in the south as it is in the north. Urban populations may be less long-term in their orientation than rural ones. Some groups possibly exhibit more tolerance of uncertainty than others. If we accept the earlier premise that India lives in three centuries simultaneously, then some degree of variance needs to be built into the model. Nevertheless it's a useful tool for identifying gaps and formulating policies to close them.

Saint Gobain has gone further and adapted the standard Hofstede model. It has added an additional dimension, named 'destiny orientation', and found it to be another area where the overlap between Saint Gobain culture and Indian culture is weak. PK puts it matter-of-factly: 'India has a strong sense of destiny. If the light bulb goes off, an Indian will says "It is destiny!" At Saint Gobain we'll ask "when was the last preventative maintenance report compiled?"'

While a general sense of optimism and confidence can be read into much of India's millennials' thinking and behaviour, PK sees a parallel reality:

> A large part of leaderships' task is to instil confidence. This generation lacks confidence. It experiences extreme peer pressure. Recognition therefore is very important. So is support to build self-esteem, the chance to lead, and to have visibility of leadership.

Other companies in India are also introducing flatter structures. They may not specifically frame this as a way of reducing 'power distance' but that will be one of its implicit paybacks. Other benefits accrue. Fewer layers make decision making and execution speedier and make it easier to get closer to customers and read markets in more granular detail without the degradation of data and insights that long chains of command produce. Businesses become more agile, productivity improves, and the bottom line gets a boost.

Vodafone repositions itself for a millennial generation

Telecoms giant Vodafone India has taken out three layers of designation in three years. The objective is to shorten the distance between decision maker and the market. It's part of a broader strategy to be more digitally enabled. Vodafone India has reached the point where more than half its employees are millennials. It understands the demographic shift as part of a set of disruptions to a sector that's seen unprecedented growth in the past decade. Challenges include the arrival of a host of exciting digital technologies that are transforming how India consumes data. Vodafone also has a hungry and hugely well-funded new competitor in Reliance Jio. The newly launched data-arm of Reliance Industries, owned by India's richest man, Mukesh Ambani, has put a boot to the backside of the telecoms market in the past year. In part as a response to that, Vodafone India is embarking on a merger with erstwhile competitor Idea.

The man charged with navigating these turbulent waters is CEO Sunil Sood, an easy-going, casually attired, 17-year veteran of India's telecoms sector. I met Sunil and Sandeep Batra, SVP – Resourcing, L&D & Talent

Figure 5.1

Management ('team leader' at Saint Gobain!). Together we discuss their transformation agenda. Days earlier the company had unveiled its new global
positioning. The old 'Power to you' tagline has been replaced with the much
more dynamic 'The future is exciting. Ready?' For Sunil that's not just a market-
facing concept, but one that must resonate internally too. That makes him a
rarity among Indian executives for whom the connection between a brand's
external voice and the employee experience is largely uncharted territory.

He says:

> The future is exciting, but it also brings fear and apprehension. How
> will I adapt and how will it affect my future are questions that our
> customers and our employees ask. Our job is to take them by the hand
> and walk them through the journey at a pace that they're comfortable
> with. Digital natives will be faster than older generations.

On the delayering Sunil tells me:

> We now get much better feedback from the field on what's happening.
> But we had to redesign the organisation to achieve that. That doesn't
> happen overnight. It took us six months. We completed a few small
> circles and we used the same style of experimentation and iterative
> process internally that we'd use for product development and we
> learned from that. Then we went out and did it nationally.

Sandeep explains that digital enablement is part of the delayering.

> A supervisor has to use digital tools because suddenly the number of
> people who report to him goes up. That gives him access to more
> information at a much more granular level. But it's also a cultural
> change because it means he has to manage in a different way that's
> more remote. We're helping people practise and use the technology. It's
> being done across the board. Customers experience it. So do our
> colleagues. People are forced to learn and operate digitally. It's not an
> easy transition but we're making that shift.

Digital technology is an enabler of Vodafone's transformation. But Sunil
and his team know that technology alone is never the answer. Alongside the
shiny new stuff that reduces some of the friction on the technology side he
sees the need for an engaged workforce. Clarity and definitiveness are
important and so is authenticity. He's done away with 'Sir' and 'Madam'
and encourages use of first names. Dress codes have been relaxed. These
may seem trivial points. But breaking down barriers to encourage openness
is an important activity on the journey of culture change.

Another aspect of the internal culture change is to promote a sense that
it's OK to fail. Culturally, in India, this is not an easy concept to propagate,

though the thriving start-up scene is a measure of the way in which attitudes are changing. Alan Rosling captures the change deftly in his book *Boom Country*.[4] Choosing to be an entrepreneur is slowly becoming more acceptable but failure, and the willingness to acknowledge it, remains a touchy subject.

Part of the Vodafone transformation is to increase the number of women in the organisation. It's made progress by almost doubling the number from 13 per cent to 25 per cent in the past three years. It aims to get to 33 per cent. But the agenda is not just about numbers. Vodafone India wants to be a place of diversity and equality. That contrasts to the day-to-day experience of many people in all other areas of their lives including the home and family, so requires more hand-holding, training, and enablement. Its pitch to prospective employees is to position itself as a technology company – and one with a purpose beyond making money. In 2013 it launched Vodafone World of Difference, an initiative that makes opportunities for staff to spend periods of four to six weeks with NGOs where they can develop their skills and make contributions to other parts of society. This is a response to a growing perception that millennials want to work for organisations with strong purpose. Deloitte's 2016 millennials survey[5] highlights this, suggesting that purpose is important for all millennials and particularly so for those in emerging markets.

But plenty of other motivations are at play when it comes to millennial expectations in the workplace.

Culture eats strategy for breakfast

Nikunj Shah is a Kenyan-born, Oxford University and INSAED-educated, British passport-holding Indian who came to India ten years ago after a stint in Mozambique. He has responsibility for family-owned manufacturing businesses in India but also allocates time and resources to a recruitment business he and wife Seema Shah founded a few years ago. They are also angel investors in start-ups so their business interests span the traditional to new age enterprises. Nikunj employs people in Mumbai and Ahmedabad and identifies a marked difference in attitudes.

> The attrition rates in a Tier 2 city are much lower. In Mumbai there's a universe of opportunities available and the aspiration is higher. By that I mean the cost of living is much greater and therefore the need to earn and the threshold at which comes security is much higher. But at the same time the number of options is exponential.

He sees success in recruiting and retaining millennial talent in terms of the organisation's ability to provide a responsive environment in which they can have a degree of autonomy and receive prompt and regular feedback. Access to capable mentors is key.

We've changed the incentive structures so they work on a quarterly basis. For older generations an annual performance target works but that time frame is too stretched for millennials. And we've moved away where possible from a command and control approach. You can't expect to keep people if you're barking orders down the line at them.

The thread running through to this section is culture. The core question is how organisations create the culture that will sustain them through this period of change. The premise is that the majority of Indian companies currently have cultures rooted in a past era. Those cultures evolved in response to scarcity, lack of opportunity, low growth, and uncertainty. They vary of course but they tend to be closed, rule bound, and risk averse. Leadership is positional. Deference is expected. An enterprise wishing to attract and co-create value with a group of young people whose frame of reference has altered needs a culture that's more agile. It needs to encourage experimentation and innovation, to be less hierarchical and more open. A shift is taking place but requires greater momentum if a true step change is to be achieved.

John Smythe is an employee engagement guru. He and I served together for a short while a decade ago on the board of the Engage Group. An invitation to speak at one of his regular Groucho Breakfasts, upstairs in Soho's storied members' club, was the genesis of this book.

John's book, *The CEO, Chief Engagement Officer: Turning Hierarchy Upside Down to Driver Performance* (Gower 2007), is summed up in this pithy paragraph:

Real engagement is based on the idea that people are more animated, creative and positive if they feel they are able to think things through for themselves and are able to add a little creativity of their own as opposed to learning by rote and complying with passed down philosophy and instructions.[6]

He describes two opposing cultures: rote learning and compliance drive one; the other encourages individuals to contribute ideas and creativity. Traditional Indian companies have a marked preference for the first. It is the antithesis of the second. The thesis at the heart of John's book is that it's the job of leaders to create the circumstances that allow the culture of ideas, creativity, and discretionary effort to take root and thrive. The key to unlock that cultural shift is engagement. I follow his lead in using the term to describe a management philosophy. It is one that strives to involve those people within the organisation who are equipped to do so, to participate in decision making. Engagement implicates people in the success of the enterprise.

In India the term generally has a different meaning. Employee engagement tends to be used in a much broader sense to describe a host of activities, sometimes recurring events requiring some level of participation. Founder's day celebration or a quiz that coincides with a religious festival might be bracketed as engagement. And of course many Indian companies sign up to some sort of annual engagement survey. Much like their contemporaries in other parts of the world, they scratch their heads and wonder what to do with the results!

John's book was published in 2007 around the time the first millennial batch, born in 1984, were entering the workforce (assuming they'd spent three years at university and had a gap year!). That may not be a coincidence. A small but fertile industry has subsequently sprouted around engagement. For some it has become a career path. Employee engagement is an important strand of that. In part that has been a reaction to the millennial mindset. Engagement is in that sense a millennial-era construct, a way of responding to the expectations of a new wave of employees. That's not to say it's only applicable to millennial-age people, but the thinking behind it is in part a response to the changes they are driving.

The engagement evolution has been most obvious in developed markets, particularly in Europe and North America. Much of the thinking and practice of engagement has been done in a cultural context different from the one I seek to describe here. As we've seen, success in India requires some level of localisation. McDonald's didn't try to convert Hindus to beef eating to sell patties. Rather its approach was to craft a menu that suited various Indian palettes. Its 'just-in-time' production methodology didn't change but the product mix did. Similarly frameworks such as the engagement model or a cultural dimensions theory need to be flexible enough to cater to a local market. Flatter organisational structures in the West make engagement an easier proposition but its chances of success are also greatly enhanced by the fact that employees have been more gradually exposed to choice and autonomy. For young Indians it's a radically different approach, and one they struggle to connect with in reality.

So then, the engagement model will need some refinement and localising if it's to deliver results in India. Not least because some of the foundations upon which it's built are tough to find. Little if anything in Indian millennial's family lives, education, or work experience will have prepared them to operate in such an environment.

As a philosophy of leadership, engagement demands willingness on the part of leaders to trust and be trusted.

Building trust

Trust is a rare commodity in India. Evidence is all around. On a day-to-day basis customers are frisked when entering a mall and asked to leave their shopping bags at the door when they walk into another shop. Institutions have an urge to over engineer processes and assume the information provided is false until proven otherwise. To get the gas pipe mended in our rented apartment I need to provide a No Objection Certificate (NOC) from the landlord before any work can be done. Documentary filmmaker Kanchi Pandya had to have her witnesses sign affidavits because the registrar wouldn't take her word on the authenticity of her marriage. Much in India is premised on mistrust and a desire to hedge.

The Tata group is India's premier business house. Indian journalists routinely coin the phrase 'salt to services' as shorthand for the interests of the 100-plus companies that bear the Tata name. Together they employ almost 700,000 people (Tata Sons, 2018).[7] Most are in India but several Tata companies now have a significant presence in other parts of the world. Visiting British politicians – of whatever hue, Leavers and Remainers, alike – rarely fail to mention that as a group Tata is now the largest manufacturing employer in the UK with around 45,000 people (*First Post*, 2014).[8] It has a unique ownership structure, the investment vehicle Tata Sons, which owns stakes in the Tata operating companies, is largely owned by charitable trusts.

Tata Chemicals is part of the globalising India story (Figure 5.2). Tata Salt regularly ranks as one of India's most trusted brands (Tata Salt, 2018),[9] giving it an enviable place of trust in hundreds of millions of kitchens. Through a series of acquisitions Tata Chemicals became the world's second largest producer of soda ash, a key ingredient for glass and detergents. It bought General Chemicals Industrial Products in the US, Brunner Mond, a legacy business of ICI in the UK, and as part of that purchase acquired Magadi Soda in Kenya. Colleagues now include miners in Green River, Wyoming, engineers in Northwich in Cheshire, England, and Kenyan managers who spend their working week at Lake Magadi in the heart of the Rift Valley before returning to their homes and families in Nairobi at

Figure 5.2

the weekend. By far its largest employee numbers remain in India and although the head office and shared services teams are Mumbai-based, the majority of staff are based outside the metros in small towns or rural areas.

Tata Chemicals' Chief Human Resources Officer is Rackanchath (R) Nanda, a breezy reformer, and on occasion tough negotiator, from the southern state of Kerala. He's had a varied career that's taken him across the country exposing him to several sectors. Mumbai is now his base for a global role.

Over the past five years he has led an HR transformation agenda allied to a shift in the company's portfolio. By selling assets in 2017 it divested businesses exposed to subsidies, such as fertilisers. It is making major investments in wellness segments such as nutraceuticals. The shift is from industrial chemicals and into more brand-led consumer products. So Nanda's challenge is two-fold. He has to respond to the arrival of millennials in the workforce and attract them into the new knowledge-based, brand-led activities. He can't alienate his traditional, longer-serving colleagues for whom change may not be palatable. He sees other modernising opportunities if the company is to keep pace in a dynamic market in which some of its traditional advantages have been eroded.

But with determination during the past five years Nanda and his boss, the managing director of Tata Chemicals Ramakrishnan Mukundan, have chipped away at old orders.

One of the foundational conversations for this book was a discussion with Nanda. He explained how most of the policies and processes that existed were built on an assumption of mistrust. That the group's place in the hearts of so many Indians is based on its reputation for trust was an irony not lost on him. 'Our policies were aimed at catching the 1 per cent of actions that shouldn't happen. We were not creating policies that would enable the 99 per cent'. Internal mechanisms were hard wired to assume individuals were out to game the system. Mistrust was the default setting. As anyone who's managed in a large organisation recognises, not only does that contaminate the culture it's also a highly inefficient and wasteful way of managing internal processes.

The leadership's pivot was to accept that in the vast majority of cases an individual's motivation is genuine. So the new policies, leave requests, expenses claims, and other day-to-day transactions are part of a broader culture change initiative branded 'Simpli5', designed to enable a speedy approval and settlement process. Individuals are enabled to take responsibility rather than waiting interminably for approvals from on high.

In these traditional engineering companies such as Saint Gobain and Tata Chemicals, the real transformation agenda is in helping middle managers understand and respond to the changes taking place around them. Nanda cites his colleagues at Mithapur, a sleepy company town on the western coast of Gujarat, birthplace of the business and where it is the only employer of significance.

You have managers who can't understand why a young person joining only wants to be on the shop floor for a couple of years and then wants to move on. Sixty per cent of those managers have children of the same age group, from the same community. Do they expect their children to stay put? No. So we have to recognise that others also want progress and that you can't have two different value systems. The kids who'll come in to work for you won't be inferior. You have to appreciate that they come from the same population and in the 2–3 years that they spend with you have to co-create value. They come in at a particular level and they go out knowing more and they still hold you as one of their mentors as a role model wherever they go. Will they say: 'This is my first boss and I'd always love to go back and work with my first boss'. Do you create that experience for them? Many managers have started to change. Their success depends on their ability to create that environment because if they don't they'll constantly be fire fighting.

The default corporate cultural setting for the majority of Indian companies has been to assume guilt and rely on command and control models. That style of non-engagement doesn't sit well with millennials.

The trust deficit was a point highlighted in my interview with EduTech entrepreneur Shoba Purushothaman. She's a co-founder of Hardskills, an online training business focused on training large numbers of emerging managers in emerging markets. Her company is addressing the skills gap among young managers – millennial by definition. In India they will, on the whole, have an excellent technical background but lack a set of what have historically been called 'soft skills': time management, presentation and communications skills, delegation, giving and receiving feedback, and others. Along with co-founder Anthony Hayward she spent several years living in India. They developed content in a classroom setting before building an online delivery platform. They have first-hand experience of working at close quarters with Indian millennials. Meanwhile their clients are Gen X HR and business unit managers in companies that are grappling with the conundrum of up-skilling their people. They will be seeking to achieve some form of culture change.

Shoba describes the prevailing culture in many traditional Indian companies based on an assumption of 'guilty 'til proven innocent'. She characterises the millennial generation as 'cynical about corporate structures and unresponsive to traditional, positional leadership'. You don't need to be Sherlock Holmes to see a connection. The cynicism impairs their prospects, she says.

Because they don't respect the leader just because of the position, they are a lot less beholden, which is good. But the cynicism means that many aren't adept at using organisational ladders as a mechanism for career advancement. For many the job is a means of generating income rather than a stepping stone towards a bigger goal.

This is a stark contrast to the earlier generations for whom the career paths were clearly marked out and a slow-moving measure of progression and advancement. Horizons, once distant, requiring endless deferred gratification, have shortened. A generation wants quick results.

Resolving the issue of trust and inserting the presumption of innocence into corporate culture is key to engaging millennials. It's a way to overturn the cynicism and a massively more efficient way of running a team, a department, business unit, or enterprise. While 'guilt' and 'innocence' are binary, there's a continuum between 'trust' and 'mistrust'. How to prepare young people to operate against that backdrop when they live in a society where mistrust is endemic? At what point are they equipped to be trusted? How to get the ones who hold the power to junk the 'guilty 'til proven' mentality?

The case of Netflix is instructive (Figure 5.3). The streaming service stole the show on trust with its take-as-much-holiday-as-you-want policy. The 'reinvention of HR', as *Harvard Business Review* (2014)[10] described Netflix's radical approach to engagement, has become the 21st-century's holy grail for people interested in the link between corporate culture and corporate earnings. Fast Company ranked Netflix the second most innovative company in the world in February 2018, at which point its market cap was more than US$100 billion (Reuters, 2018).[11]

Many great ideas reside in the document that Patty McCord, then Netflix chief talent officer, and CEO Reed Hastings wrote to explain the thinking behind their path-breaking, but really quite simple philosophy. The one that

Figure 5.3

caught the millennial *Zeitgeist* was that employees were able to 'take whatever time-off they felt was appropriate'. The wording is more nuanced in reality than in the myth it's perpetuated.

The Netflix approach to people includes five tenets: Hire, Reward, and Tolerate Only Fully Formed Adults; Tell the Truth about Performance; Managers Own the Job of Creating Great Teams; Leaders Own the Job of Creating the Company Culture; and Good Talent Managers Think Like Businesspeople and Innovators First, and Like HR People Last. It's brilliant: as millennial as Kygo's dance music. Crucially at the heart of these principles is a healthy assumption of trust.

Would this *laissez faire* approach work in India where even getting people into the office by 10 am is a challenge?

I posed the question to Heather Saville Gupta, an experienced HR professional with an international perspective. She jettisoned the trappings of life in London's media circus at the turn of the millennium in search of adventure. Mumbai has been her home for 15 years. As well as raising two children, being part of the successful growth and sale of UTV to Disney, she found time to write a fictionalised account of cross-cultural dating and marriage in the Maximum City (2013).[12]

She describes HR management in India at this moment as 'herding millennials'. Given that most HR professionals anywhere in the world are currently focused on millennials, it's the term 'herding' that captures my interest. 'In the past employees were somewhat more respectful of the processes like an appraisal system. They recognised a need to wait for promotion. Attrition was always there but not because they just need to leave', she says.

Her experience has been in media, a sector perhaps more likely to be forward thinking when it comes to HR policy than the traditional engineering and manufacturing companies. Would a Netflix-style trust-based model work in Indian companies?

Her response, a definitive No!

> The model only works if people have self-regulation. Note the principle of only hiring fully formed adults. Young Indians lack that self-regulation because their lives have always been managed for them. Even millennials still want the formality because they can't make decisions and take ownership of things.

Many young Indians still live at home until they marry – and men often then bring their wife to the family home. It means lots of the life skills that one would find in their western contemporaries are absent. They have not had to make their own financial decisions. Their shoulders have not had to bear the burden of responsibility. As Raj, the train-riding travel editor, notes, many of his peers feel unqualified to make their own choice of life partner. They don't trust themselves in private so it's probably unreasonable to expect them to do so in public.

The response should not be to fall back on command and control and assume guilt rather than innocence. The alternative is to carefully build the confidence that is needed to manage the trust. The point was made earlier by PK. Openness and transparency are a good starting point.

Building performance-led cultures

While dubious about the take-as-much-holiday-as-you-want approach, Heather does see great merit in the second tenet: 'Tell the Truth about Performance'. That she sees as a positive and meaningful step along the trust continuum in an Indian context. She says:

> I'm refreshed by the fact that the feet touching, forelock-tugging culture is disappearing from Indian corporate culture. The story you have to tell these people coming in is that it's not about seniority and hitting all those milestones. You will be rewarded for your performance.

Yet that too is an unsettling notion for many. Seeing performance as a metric of career progression, either for themselves or for their charges, remains a novel idea for many managers. The fatalism of Hinduism informs much thinking. If we're destined to have many lives then why stress too much about hitting some arbitrary performance measure in this one. It's not like my job depends upon it. Better luck next time around!

Many Indian employees think about their workplace contribution in terms of their inputs and not the resulting output. They struggle to see their performance in terms of what they deliver – because that's not traditionally been the measure. Some business leaders see the value but struggle against cultures that have other foundations and beliefs.

In organisations where promotions are based on length of tenure rather than performance it becomes almost impossible to leapfrog colleagues. The idea of an older person reporting to a younger one goes against the grain on many levels. Neither party is really ready, nor has the skills, to manage that situation. And that stymies businesses. It robs them of new and novel ideas and perpetuates compliance with what John Smythe described as 'passed down philosophy'. How can a business develop and market products that will appeal to millennial consumers if it doesn't put millennials in decision-making roles?

Of course one of the points of this book is to acknowledge that some of these things are changing.

Bernadine Swamy is a 20-year veteran of the HR practice in India. In that time she's managed across various disciplines in tech and financial services organisations. Currently she serves as group head of HR for WPP companies in India. She's seen many changes but the shift towards performance recognition, while nascent, is one of the most important, she tells me.

There are an increasing number of performance-oriented businesses in which it's possible to leapfrog your boss and end up as a manager of people that may be significantly older. It's a trend – the biggest change I've seen in my 20 years in HR. It's not consistent with a traditional Indian mindset which is focused on hierarchy and tenure and seniority. We're getting there!

She observes and comments on the resilience of positional leadership, but an area where in two decades she's seen some change. 'In some more forward-looking organisations, typically the performance-oriented ones, we're seeing a shift towards situational leadership styles'.

She describes the young people she's now recruiting as 'highly ambitious' but acknowledges that the organisation has 'high expectations' too. She says:

Those expectations are made clear so that there's an alignment. If I explain in the beginning he or she knows what has to be done to bridge the gap. It starts with openness in communications. We're getting better at managing expectations about behaviour as well as tasks.

Authenticity in leadership

A culture in which leaders communicate openly and, to coin the Netflix terminology, 'Tell the Truth about Performance' is fundamental to engagement. In an Indian context, leaders will be thought of as senior executives. In the engagement model I describe, 'leaders' includes all who have a role to lead whether at supervisory and team head level, department manager, or business unit honcho. Open communication requires trust to have been established and must be managed carefully. That's particularly so in a culture where openness and directness are rarely practised. Giving and receiving feedback are not core competencies. In response to that gap Hardskills includes giving and receiving feedback in its global business skills programme. That is, as part of a broader drive to enable greater self-awareness. Without self-awareness the move from positional to situational leadership styles is doomed.

Perhaps unsurprisingly the examples of open communication are more common than, though not restricted to, less traditional industry sectors. Some are a management response to the increasingly prevalent millennial mindset. Others are emerging organically.

Onkar, managing director of Austere Analytics in Bangalore, didn't use the term engagement when I met him, but he described it as he spoke about the open culture as the centrepiece of his management philosophy. By meeting face-to-face with his team fortnightly he's built their trust. His communication style is open and direct and he expects that to be reciprocated. He clearly understands that creating the company culture is central to his leadership style. He's modelling the behaviour he wants to see. Leading from the front and practising what he preaches he's been rewarded with low attrition rates and a highly engaged team prepared to make discretionary effort. It's worth remembering they came in to the office on a holiday to meet me and be interviewed. Leaders in larger established businesses may say it's easier to perpetuate a culture in a small, young business. They're right. But the culture he's propagating gives him a competitive advantage in the battle for talent and makes him an employer of choice. He's already poaching staff from much larger competitors and his recruits identify his open style as a winning way. To replicate his success, large organisations need to heed the Netflix mantra 'Managers Own the Job of Creating Great Teams'. Pushing ownership down the line, empowering those who lead small groups builds a context in which they too can replicate this open style of communication.

Heather gives me another example of openness in action. She's just promoted a 25-year-old guy into a team leader position. She waited for a while and coached him to build on his competency and add some much needed maturity and communications skills. But it wasn't just him who was affected by the promotion. She considered its impact on other team members. She says:

> I called in one of his peers. She's a couple of years older and we're also coaching her. I knew that she'd have a response to his promotion. So I sat her down and said, 'Before it's been announced I want you to know. I know you'll have a response and I know what that will be. But you need to understand that you have a path and it's a different one and we've made that clear. I want you to see this in that context'. And she had never been dealt with in that manner but she could see that this was an example of transparency in action.

She adds:

> It's very important not just to have values and to communicate those but to identify behaviours that are consistent with that value and to be seen to recognise and reward those behaviours. I find that with coaching and counselling millennials respond very well to that clarity and definitiveness.

We met Rickshaw's boss Mahua Hazarika earlier and her new hire Stacy Samuels in the previous chapter. The company's studio is a converted industrial space in Goregaon in Mumbai's western suburbs. Low rents and relative accessibility make it a popular destination for creative and tech start-ups. Tattooed hipsters sip *chai* and munch *vada pav* (a carb-fest of fried potato and bread roll), and smoke cigarettes at the ramshackle stalls in the tight lanes. Fashion shoots take place in the crumbling buildings that echo a past era of textile industry now making way for a new wave of enterprise. Rickshaw's space could be a creative agency almost anywhere in the world – open-plan, post-industrial exposed walls and rows of iMacs on long workbenches.

Mahua previously had a career in the drinks industry. Quitting the booze, professionally, nearly a decade ago she moved into agency life. Her leadership style is clear and definitive.

Eighty per cent of her staff are millennials, they come from across the social strata. Most are not originally from Mumbai but like moths are drawn to the flickering screens and nocturnal buzz, the rhythm of India's advertising world. Some appear unannounced as I interview her. Polite and precise they are unencumbered by deference.

Does she recognise the description of millennials as an entitled generation, hungry for rapid progress and lacking loyalty?

> Yes. And it's a damn good thing. They thrive on challenges. We throw them in at the deep end. We are conscious of the fact that they'll only stay for two or three years. We make the most of it. The goals we set are stringent and clear from day one. And we're transparent that the horizon is three years. We manage them in, through, and out.

Finding creatively minded talent is tough in a country where engineering, medicine, and accountancy have been valued and rote learning predominates in classrooms. 'We have young Indians coming out of college with great memories but who struggle to "think outside the box". I want them to demolish the bloody box', she says. So how to find talent? She lectures frequently and offers multiple internships to eager graduates. 'But ultimately you have to grow your own'. Lateral hires don't work out.

> We always fail when we bring in senior talent from outside because their mindset is more to do with hierarchy and incremental progress. I've stopped taking senior people in my discipline. I'd rather have young people vying for the positions.

Social media has changed the landscape for recruiting managers and candidates and opened up new pipelines of talent and alternative pathways into employment. It's also adding transparency, around salaries and working conditions for example, that didn't previously exist. Glassdoor, the website that allows employees and former employees to rate their experience of working for companies, seems to have its finger on the pulse of Indian corporate life and gives both employers and employees an additional source of information and perspective. It's another way in which millennial-era technology, combined with a mindset based on merit rather than deference, is transforming institutions and demanding greater levels of authenticity.

A corporate culture that allowed 'shady behaviour' and where her boss was ill equipped to provide the level of leadership she required meant Sureka quit. Whether she's in India, the UK, or the US she has plenty of options available to her. Failure to get to grips with the culture conundrum means missing out on high-potential talent.

Talent acquisition

Though STEM subjects have been favoured by large numbers of Indians the struggles that agency boss Mahua described in finding the right talent aren't restricted to creative services. Indian institutions enrol almost 3 million technology and engineering students and turn out around 1.5 million engineering graduates every year (*India Today*, 2016).[13] Graduate employability has long been a concern for Indian employers. The skills gap is profound. One study put the number of engineering graduates ready to make a meaningful contribution to the economy at a paltry 7 per cent (Aspiring Minds, 2016).[14] This makes the task of those recruiting managers sent out to interview and make campus offers a challenging one.

For the past five years Kalpana Medbalmi has been in charge of campus recruitment for Quinnox, a Chicago-headquartered tech services company. The bulk of its workforce is in India where it recruits 70–100 graduate engineers every year. It focuses its efforts on around 50 institutes in Mumbai and Bangalore.

Basic technical competence, judged by exam results is a prerequisite and in relative profusion. What Kalpana and her team are looking for in prospective hires is good communications skills, adaptability, willingness to learn. These are lacking in many candidates she says. Technical skills may be on a par with candidates from both Mumbai and Bangalore. But she notes a significant difference in the other competencies. 'Students from Mumbai are more advanced in the soft skills'. She also experiences much higher drop out rates with those who join Quinnox teams in Bangalore. 'Dropout rates are higher because as a tech hub Bangalore offers more opportunities and we face more competition'.

The number of career choices for graduate engineers has blossomed in the past 10–15 years. And the number of channels, including social media and networking sites, by which they can access those opportunities has exploded.

Kalpana's response has been to take a more strategic approach to engaging with her target institutions and seeking to differentiate Quinnox as an employer of choice. She cites a number of activities.

> We're judged on our recruitment practices, our past recruitment actions, the way we integrate and train joiners and the degree to which

we can successfully deploy them. So whereas in the past campus recruitment was seen as a one off, annual activity we've come to think of it as a continual process. Our relationship with universities doesn't end. So we're engaging students and placement committee members on a more regular basis. We communicate more, share success stories – tell them who was a star from the last batch – pass on client appreciations. We have technical people invested in that process, not just HR. Those colleagues are able to talk about the reality of projects, domain opportunities, software applications, and what a career path might look like. So the university connect has become much more important to us. It's about brand building, developing relationships with faculty members, and helping them build their knowledge of our expectations.

She observes a greater confidence in the recent crops of graduates who have mapped out career paths for themselves including the technologies and domains within which they want to learn and grow their careers.

Even seven or eight years ago we had to do a lot of probing to understand their expectations. That's changed – again because of their access to networks and channels through which they can get real-time information about us and our competitors.

Workplace matchmakers

As professional matchmakers, recruitment consultants acquire an intimate knowledge of both sides of the hiring equation. To be successful they have to understand the culture of their client organisations. They learn what will work and what will not, and where some compromise is needed to find common ground. If they can't make the right pairings, they find they're back on the market touting their own CVs.

Julia Manke is one who's honed the skills. A former McKinsey analyst she undertook assignments in the US, UK, and India before becoming a businesswoman and setting up Fingertips, a recruitment business, 12 years ago. Softly spoken, she's an active listener and has a good ear both for the things her clients are seeking in candidates and what the prospective hires she interviews expect from a job. She's attuned to the degree candidates are prepared for the world of work. 'The gulf in expectations is huge', she tells me.

As a result she spends significant time coaching both parties in order to manage misaligned expectations and bridge that gap.

On the candidate's side I meet people who don't know what they're looking for and have no understanding of what an employer may want from them. They need to have a deeper understanding of what the world of work demands. On the client's side I meet people who have a millennial son or daughter of their own and they know their traits and are willing to respond to them in a fairly mature way. But they're unwilling to accept the same in an employee.

In the past a 'do as I say, not what I do' attitude may have been sustained by the power of positional leadership. Millennials seeking authenticity will take exception to this inconsistency.

The gap has widened in a decade. 'Ten years ago a 20-year old was desperate to find a job and then to hold onto it. Now I see a generation in their early 20s who are neither fearful of not finding a job nor of losing one'. What engages them? She says that while money is a factor it's often the opportunity to be involved early, to have access to founding leaders and play a role in establishing something new that appeals to a younger generation. The credibility and past success that established businesses see as a cornerstone of their pulling power holds much less sway now.

The changing attitudes to work we're experiencing in India are opening a new revenue stream for recruitment consultants. As the notion of the job for life and the certainty that came with it fades, there's a growing market for lateral hires.

Lateral hiring is a challenge for organisations because it involves bringing in 'outsiders' and the ability to accommodate them within the prevailing culture. Historically, there was of course some, but less of this type of movement within the workforce. While it's a boon to the recruitment community, it introduces new complexities for business leaders who haven't previously had to manage so much inbound or outbound traffic.

Reading between the lines of my conversations with headhunters and recruiters I sense that there's a gap within hiring organisations between the business leaders and their HR partners. With notable exceptions it seems that HR functions have been slower to respond to the new era of millennial employees than have their business sponsors. HR is in many instances failing to keep up and recruiters are finding their services in increasing demand in a market that's becoming more dynamic and multi-layered. Conventional policies and practices will have to change further if India's large organisations are to compete with the nimbler, flatter, digital-native competitors.

Key takeaways

1 **See the world through their eyes.** The Greek philosopher Epictetus is credited with saying: 'We have two ears and one mouth so that we can listen twice as much as we speak'. As a principle it's rarely applied in India. At home, in school, in the workplace people (particularly the young, and women, and those seen as lower down the pecking order) are accustomed to being talked at, instructed, and interrogated. Their context is different. Listening will help you understand and build a picture through their eyes. Don't assume that their cultural frame of

reference coincides with yours. Their world looks different. They may feel overwhelmed with opportunity, fearful, wildly (and sometimes unrealistically) confident, or out of their depth.

Encourage them to use their own words. Let them set the agenda. Hear what they say, and crucially what they leave out.

Use the principles of Appreciative Inquiry. A strength-based methodology it's used primarily in the professional field of change management. At its heart is a desire to see each other and ourselves at our best – our most engaged. Rather than looking at problems it seeks out the times and places when we've achieved great things. The goal is to capture and replicate those moments more frequently. As a tool to get into 'other peoples shoes' it has much to recommend it.

2   **Assume innocence and enable rather than police.** 'Command and control' has its roots in the military. It's highly regulated and presumes a degree of mistrust. As a workplace culture it militates against experimentation and individual risk taking. Plenty of organisations say they want their employees to show entrepreneurial spirit. Some go as far as to write it into the vision, mission, and values statements and then hang it on the walls of their toilets. Putting people under surveillance won't unleash their creative passions.

Seek to nurture environments in which trust is the default setting and be clear about the boundaries. Encourage them to take risks and to learn from those. Entrepreneurs do it all the time. It requires a culture in which it's alright to fail. This is a big challenge in the Indian context. At school kids are asked why did you drop five marks, not congratulated for getting 95 per cent. In the workplace there's a fondness for raking over failures rather than celebrating success.

An enabling culture will involve plenty of open and honest communication. It will value performance. Acceptable behaviours will be role-modelled by leaders. Unacceptable behaviour will be called out. Emphasis will be given to outputs rather than inputs. Employees will have access to leaders, regularly and in authentic settings.

Don't invest in systems to check compliance at the expense of value creation. Use technology as an enabler. Let digital technology simplify and speed up processes. Let people use the devices they already have in their hand to manage their daily routines and transactions.

3   **Make the employment period time bound.** Accept that some employees will want to build their careers faster than can be achieved within your organisation. Too often this is portrayed as a lack of loyalty. It isn't. Think about the alumni networks of high-performing organisations. They relish the contributions of former colleagues who've moved on. Loyalty shouldn't be seen as length of tenure but about the contribution that's made.

Leaders can fret about attrition rates going up. Or they can think about co-creating the maximum value in a designated time period. This requires a change of mindset within the organisation because it necessitates a higher level of participation from managers. Time is set aside to discuss and agree development plans. Progress is reviewed at regular intervals against an agreed set of objectives and mapped. Success is acknowledged. Mistakes and failures are deconstructed and analysed. Lessons are learned and shared. Stretch projects are completed. Open communication is vital. Team leader and team member must be able to give and receive feedback. Trust must be in ample supply. Both company and employee will learn much and, if managed dextrously, all parties see and understand the co-created value.

The approach resonates with the millennial mindset. It does nothing to thwart their ambitions. It has a welcome level of transparency, which sets the scene well for other constructive interactions. And make sure you have great ways to keep in touch once they've moved on. Invite them back to share their stories with the next crop. Celebrate their next success. Build your own influential, and loyal, alumni network.

4   **Be precise. Don't fudge.** Indians' willingness to deal with ambiguity and complexity becomes a self-fulfilling prophecy. Obfuscation creates inefficiency. It leads to misunderstanding. Strive to use terms that are unambiguous. Speak and write in simple language. Observe the principle of less is more (but avoid the use of acronyms). Address issues directly and promptly. Don't leave discussions unresolved.

Set clear goals with realistic deadlines. Be precise about objectives and measures of success. Learn to describe what good looks like. Insist on precise timekeeping – not just in terms of when things start but when they end, too.

5   **Hire for cultural fit.** Of course technical skills need to be in place. That's not what's going to define your best employees. Look for people who share your values. Build networks in the places where they congregate.

Understand the type of organisation you are and the culture you want to promote. Map it. Write it down. Have stories that you can share with potential recruits about the way you work. Explain how things are done around here. Use tests that uncover their 'soft skills' and make that part of the scoring process.

6   **Embrace authenticity and transparency.** Don't allow two sets of values to exist. Be consistent. Be honest – if you don't have an answer, say so.

Authenticity is a trait that the millennial mindset values and managers should work to achieve that. Let people understand how their efforts contribute to the overall objective. Be open about progress towards that objective.

7   **'More I, less we'.** Acres of rainforests have been sacrificed to publish the countless books that exhort business leaders to build corporate cultures that replace 'I' with 'we'. We're endlessly encouraged to abandon our

'silos' and to take a 'holistic' view. 'There's no "I" in team!' says the leadership coach.

In Indian organisations, there's a compelling need to turn that advice on its head. India's low score for individualism is indicative of a collective ability to not shoulder responsibility. Greater levels of personal account- ability are required.

Seek to implicate individuals in the success of the enterprise. Be clear – as part of an open communication style – about where individual con- tribution fits in the overall scheme of things. Work hard to create a culture of personal accountability. Millennials are more and more inclined to 'I' but their frames of reference both in families, school, college, and almost every other social institution mean they are ill equipped or willing to take ownership of their own destinies. Meet face-to-face, one-on-one, regularly and encourage others to follow suit. Set unambiguous goals. Reward success and broadcast success stories. Be seen to take ownership and be accountable for your own failures as well as successes. Measure individual performance. Mentor and coach individuals to build their confidence. It encourages greater autonomy and creates a virtuous circle. Make collaboration an activity in which the sum of the whole is greater than the sum of the parts but reward individual contributions.

Push people to become specialists in key activities. Build best-of-breed teams where individuals have clear roles and responsibilities.

Notes

1 *The Economic Times*, 9 June 2017. Tata Motors scraps designations to create a flatter organisation, boost creativity. Available at https://economictimes. indiatimes.com/industry/tata-motors-scraps-designations-to-create-a-flatter- organisation-boost-creativity/articleshow/59060469.cms. Accessed on 21/09/ 2018.
2 *The Hindu Business Line*, 2017. Flat response: Tata Motors brings back designations. Available at www.thehindubusinessline.com/companies/flat- response-tata-motors-brings-back-designations/article9791248.ece. Accessed on 23/07/2018.
3 *Forbes*, 2017. India's millennials to drive growth in four key sectors. Available at www.forbes.com/sites/morganstanley/2017/06/23/indias-millennials-to-drive- growth-in-four-key-sectors/#7c1ac2334f27. Accessed on 23/07/2018.
4 Roslin A, 2017. *Boom Country: The New Wave of Indian Entrepreneurship*, Hachette India.
5 Deloitte, 2016. The 2016 Deloitte millennial survey. Available at www2. deloitte.com/content/dam/Deloitte/global/Documents/About-Deloitte/gx-millen ial-survey-2016-exec-summary.pdf. Accessed on 23/07/2018.
6 Smythe J, 2007. *The CEO Chief Engagement Officer: Turing Hierarchy Upside Down to Driver Performance*, Gower.

7 Tata Sons, 2018. Tata group financials. Available at www.tata.com/htm/Group_Investor_GroupFinancials.htm#employees. Accessed on 23/07/2018.

8 *First Post*, 2014. Brand India shines: Tata is UK's biggest industrial employer. Available at www.firstpost.com/business/thank-tata-brand-india-takes-on-more-shine-in-uk-84141.html. Accessed on 23/07/2018.

9 Tata Salt, 2018. About us. Available at www.tatasalt.com/about-us. Accessed on 23/07/2018.

10 *Harvard Business Review*, 2014. How Netflix reinvented HR. Available at https://hbr.org/2014/01/how-netflix-reinvented-hr. Accessed on 23/07/2018.

11 Reuters, 2018. Netflix crosses $100 billion market capitalization as subscribers surge. Available at www.reuters.com/article/us-netflix-results/netflix-crosses-100-billion-market-capitalization-as-subscribers-surge-idUSKBN1FB2WM. Accessed on 23/07/2018.

12 Saville Gupta H, 2013. *Becoming Mrs Kumar*, Penguin India.

13 *India Today*, 2016. Only 7 per cent engineering graduates employable: what's wrong with India's engineers? Available at http://indiatoday.intoday.in/education/story/engineering-employment-problems/1/713827.html. Accessed on 23/07/2018.

14 Aspiring Minds, 2016. National employability report. Available at www.aspiringminds.com/sites/default/files/National%20Employability%20Report%20-%20Engineers%20Annual%20Report%202016.pdf. Accessed on 23/07/2018.

6 Brands that capture the millennial mindset

As acts of subversion go, buying a sofa doesn't rank high, but there's something oddly subversive about Pepperfry.com, an Indian online furniture store flogging a warehouse-worth of household products every day. Its website offers a choice of almost 1,000 sofas (Figure 6.1).

Founded in 2011, Pepperfry is quietly disrupting several tenets of traditional Indian culture. It challenges established spending patterns and places choice in the hands of the young, gives autonomy and offers instant gratification. In the past spending on big-ticket items such as furniture, electrical appliances, vehicles, and gold was sanctioned during religious festivals as part of a seasonal glut of retail activity. Patriarchs made decisions with their fingers firmly looped in the purse strings as part of a programme of carefully orchestrated household expenditure. Now young people, setting up home in greater numbers than ever before, more mobile and wealthier, are taking control for themselves. No need to wait until Diwali or Eid. No need to ask permission. A treasure chest of household goods lies a click away. The company claims it makes a sale every 25 seconds. Easy payment terms are available and Pepperfry even offers rental options to meet the needs of peripatetic newly minted millennials. Backed by a heavy advertising campaign in early 2012 it was an almost overnight success and has become a fixture and fitting of modern Indian life. It aims to 'help build 20 million beautiful homes by 2020' according to CMO Kashyap Vadapalli (ET Brand Equity, 2018).[1] Such an ambitious agenda is an indication of the immense scale of the opportunity in a market segment growing at speed (TechSci Research, 2014)[2] and ripe for formalisation.

'Happy furniture to you', the company's tagline says. The onus is squarely placed on the act of purchase rather than the time of celebration. The implicit message, 'take control, buy anytime, get instant gratification', is subversive in an Indian context. It sends strong signals to millennials who want independence and autonomy but aren't in the business of rebellion. The sensibilities of an older generation are not offended, even as Pepperfry pulls the rug from under them and enables a generation to subvert the traditional power and control of their elders.

Figure 6.1

Another way of looking at Pepperfry's success as an online retailer is in the context of 'Jobs Theory', or more correctly the 'Jobs-to-be-Done' Theory.

The brainchild of Harvard Business School professor Clayton Christensen, Jobs Theory is a way of looking at market opportunities by considering why a consumer looks to 'hire' a particular product to accomplish a 'job to be done'. It assumes that very often products are designed and then improved against a set of parameters that are not directly correlated to the job that the customer actually needs to get done. In their co-authored 2016 book *Competing against Luck* Christensen and his colleagues use the example of McDonald's milkshakes (*Harvard Business Review*, 2016),[3] hired by customers to do the job of getting them through a long morning drive to the office. When seen from that perspective the competition for milkshakes comes not just from other brands of milkshakes but also from a host of other food and beverage products including chocolate bars, coffee, doughnuts, and bananas. And when competing against those other types of product suddenly the size of the potential milkshake market is much bigger than previously thought.

IKEA, the world's leading furniture shop, has been brilliant at getting hired to get a job done when that job is to economically furnish an apartment. Generations of young urban professionals in much of the world, who don't want the hassle of shopping in a multitude of outlets for individual pieces to make liveable a rented apartment, have turned to the Swedish giant. In the process they made its late founder one of the world's wealthiest men. IKEA finally opened a store in India in mid-2018 with a flagship outlet in the fast-growing city of Hyderabad. It has sourced from India for three decades and claims that more than 400,000 people are employed indirectly through its supply chain (IKEA, 2018).[4] Until now its products have not been sold directly. In IKEA's absence Pepperfry has been able to provide the solution for a job to be done. The alternative involves having to engage craftsmen to make furniture or to trek across vast distances to find specialist shops, which may or may not have stock, to negotiate individually on items and then probably arrange delivery and haggle over payment. Increasingly, as Christensen and team point out in *Competing against Luck*, customers will pay a premium to have the job done in an effective manner. Pepperfry is doing what IKEA has done for decades and made a daunting and dirty job more palatable. But it goes further in terms of the customer experience in that it doesn't require the customer to head to an out-of-town warehouse, drag the furniture home, and then figure out the instructions while searching for the missing screw as they do the assembly. Pepperfry delivers and sends a person to put together the furniture. The service model is neatly tailored to Indians' expectations of delivery and outsourcing of manual tasks. Whereas in the developed markets consumers are often willing to pay a premium for a service that takes stress from their life – like paying for parking – it's evident from any time spent in India that many people will put up with high levels of discomfort to save relatively small amounts of money. One aspect of the millennial mindset seems to be a greater willingness to attribute value to an activity or service if it minimises complexity and makes a transaction smoother. The willingness to pay a convenience fee to book a cinema ticket or place a food order online is an example. And because so much of India, from its unorganised retail environment to its infrastructure and financial services sector, is inherently inconvenient there are myriad opportunities to formalise and find 'jobs to be done' that can attract a premium.

Pepperfry also addresses another job to be done and one that's key to understanding and addressing the needs of Indian millennials. Alongside the functional activity of delivering a place to sit and watch Netflix it does another important psychosocial job. It does the job of offering the young Indian control, giving the ability to claim a modicum of individuality and the chance to express themselves without doing anything that ostracises them from the social group. One of the vital jobs to be done for Indian millennials is to find autonomy without rebelling. Other brands discussed in this section manage to achieve that equilibrium, the balance of tradition and modernity in uniquely Indian ways. Getting it right with this generation is bound up in the ability to find that balance. To find jobs to be done that address psychological and social needs even if they're not stated or even acknowledged.

By using that frame of reference, that Pepperfry's 'job to be done' is one of empowering autonomy, then we can conclude that its competition doesn't just come from other furniture sellers. It competes with other brands that also meet the millennial need for freedom, independence, and social status.

Café Coffee Day's success is also in part because of its ability to identify a 'job to be done' and provide a solution. CCD, as it's ubiquitously called, celebrated its 20th anniversary in 2016. It's a millennial brand through and through. Late one evening, on one of my first visits to India, I was taken to a newly opened branch by my cousins-in-law for dessert. The experience stuck with me because it felt different from my other restaurant experiences in India. There was a nascent sense of brand, an identity and a coherence, that bound together the various parts of the experience. I've visited hundreds of times in the past decade at various times of the day often to get a job done that isn't to buy a coffee.

In the past two decades CCD has become the largest organised retail café chain in the country. There are more than 1,600 branches across the country that as well as selling coffee and sandwiches get hired by Indian millennials to do another important job. Crucially they provide a place for young people to meet away from the prying eyes of parents and other elders. A street-side tea stand will do the job of providing a hot beverage at a much lower cost, but without the privacy or social setting, or for some sense of status that a café provides. The café's job is to meet the customers' need for a 'hang out' space. Millions of first dates have taken place in CCD. Unpretentious it offers value for money. When measured against a global benchmark the service lacks finesse but that's not the quotient by which its target clientele are making their decisions. The young (and young at heart) flock to it and its appeal cuts across social groups. Millionaire property developers sit side-by-side with impoverished students. For a generation that's grown up post 1991 CCD is a familiar, authentic, and welcoming high street presence. Customers use it to do a host of jobs. It also serves decent coffee.

Several factors distinguish millennial consumers in emerging economies including India from their more affluent contemporaries in more developed markets. Engaging young Indians requires some sense of their difference both to international peers and to the generations that came before them. Many sentiments expressed by Indian millennials are consistent with those of their international peers. The willingness to invest in experiences over assets, the trend to rent rather than buy, readiness to challenge established norms and structures, shorter horizons, and desire for instant gratification, all are broadly common. Other factors are unique to India and its current moment of transformation. Brands aspiring to engage young Indian consumers must be attuned to local nuances and understand their context and the complexity within which they live and make decisions. The act of buying a sofa becomes subversive in the Indian context because it challenges an established mode of decision making and represents a new type of consumer experience. It illustrates the opportunity presented by the shift from tradition to modernity, the formalising of the informal and the value to be created by finding 'jobs to be done'.

Emerging-market consumers are on average younger than their western peers. Sixty-five per cent of Indians are under 35 years. A high proportion, therefore, are also newer consumers. Less experienced, in many cases they are taking tentative steps into the world of consumerism. Purchasing patterns are not hardwired. Choice is a more fluid, dynamic process. A young woman's smartphone may well be her first, rather than an upgrade or replacement. A householder buying a sofa, washing machine, or fridge, a scooter, a car, life insurance, or package holiday may not have done so before. His decision-making process is different to that of a veteran shopper who's satisfied the need many times before and has a store of experience to inform his choice. Jumping between brands is common and in some instances switching categories will happen when the job to be done is to acquire autonomy. So in that sense, both the Royal Enfield Bullet (see below) and the Pepperfry sofa may be doing the same job.

The thesis underlying this essay is that the 'delta of change' is greater in India than has been seen elsewhere in the world. By that I mean that the rate and distance to travel is unprecedented. In 'developed markets' citizens have experienced and participated in a series of evolutionary transformations over the past seven decades since the end of the Second World War. Millennials in developed markets have therefore been part of a more organic process of rolling change that's been going on for generations. The options available to them have evolved over time. The habits they have learned are informed by a much longer exposure and greater accessibility to a wide choice of brands. In India a paradigm shift is taking place. The changes, ushered in by the economic reforms of the early 1990s, were seismic. The key that unlocked the floodgates was economic but the disruption has been felt in almost every area of life. Millennials are deluged by myriad new choices that have arrived all at once. Multiple forces have combined. The arrival of foreign imports; local entrepreneurship driven by market economics, greater availability of funding, and a new social acceptability of risk taking; rising incomes; and a freeing of deeply embedded constraints all create a perfect storm. In this heady rush young, inexperienced consumers have few reference points on which to draw. They're excited by the potential but at the same time restrained by tradition and apprehensive.

The new influencers

Millennials' influencers are changing in this moment of flux, matching, in some manner, the changes in the west. Traditional media plays less of a role than in past generations and word-of-mouth and therefore social media have become highly influential. Conventional authority figures are being replaced though there is evidence that in emerging economies families remain important parties in decision making. McKinsey & Co.'s report on the mega prospects of emerging markets suggests that product recommendations from friends or family are more important for consumers in emerging markets than for those in the US or Britain (McKinsey & Co., 2012).[5] In part this can be put down to the much greater availability of trusted sources of reliable market data in developed markets while emerging markets still experience what Taron Khanna and Krishna Palepu describe in their book *Winning in Emerging Markets* (Harvard Business School, 2010)[6] as 'institutional voids' or the absences of market intermediaries. They propose identifying and filling those voids as a strategy for growth in emerging markets. Examples of indigenous brands that have done so in India include the billion-dollar unicorn, Paytm, which has put mobile payment in the pockets of around a quarter of a billion Indians, and food-ordering app Zomato (see below). CreditMate has created a market place as an inter-mediary between finance and second-hand motorcycles. The website Car-wale has formalised the business of buying a second-hand car and built trust in a space where it was lacking. The importance of word-of-mouth and family recommendations also reflects the prevailing lack of trust that permeates Indian society. Successful intermediaries fill that void and, as the examples above suggest, can use the voids as the foundations for new business models.

The more experienced nature of consumers in developed markets and therefore the relative sophistication of marketing professionals plays a part. In a command economy there's much less demand for those skills so the capabilities don't breed and the pool of talent is reduced. That situation has changed in the past 25 years.

Amrit Thomas, a former Hindustan Unilever (HUL) sales and marketing honcho, and now CMO at Diageo is an example. He's built his career in that period. He describes the shift in sources of knowledge and authority figures thus:

> The belief systems of young Indians are moulded not just by teachers and parents but by peer groups, social networks, and the internet. The first time they hear an item of news it happens through their news feeds and social media. Their relationship with traditional media is going to be very different. We (pre-millennial generations) grew up with a belief that what was written in newspapers and books was true. Millennials are growing up with a belief that says 'what I see on the net or what I search for on Google is fact'. Relationships with traditional sources of news and information have changed quite dramatically.

The millennial relationship with media and power and the nature of status is changing. Social media allows each to present a 'sanitised' or curated version of his of her life for public consumption and the internet allows each person to question received wisdom at the tap of a screen. Against this backdrop the messaging used to engage millennials needs to be more nuanced than traditional advertising has been. In India the *modus operandi* of most advertising, and brand communications in general, has been to bring on board a movie star as 'brand ambassador' and have them promote the brand on the assumption that their star status will translate into sales. There's seemingly been no need or incentive to connect the personality with the brand they promote in terms of values or relevance. That model doesn't resonate with young audiences, who are more values-driven and wanting authenticity. So the task for communications professionals is to find the balance to send messages that attract millennials while not offending more traditional sensibilities.

Amrit does that in a category with which India has a complex, even schizophrenic relationship. Four states in India currently have total prohibition of alcohol. In Bihar booze production is a capital offence and in 2017, a year after the ban was introduced, two brothers were sentenced to five years' jail time each for drinking alcohol (Scroll.in, 2017).[7] Illicit moonshine manufacture is rampant. Smugglers abound. The exchequer is denied vast tax revenue and many deaths are caused by consumption of unregulated bootleg liquor. Alcohol advertising is banned across the country so drinks makers have to find innovative ways to promote their products. These tend to include associations with, and sponsorship of, events, surrogate advertising (booze branded music CDs and water are two current examples), and editorial content. Packaging design plays an important role in a so-called dark market. Black Dog, an imported Scotch whisky blended in India, is one of Diageo's top selling brands in India. It was the fastest growing whisky brand in the world in the five years from 2008 to 2013 (*The Times of India*, 2013).[8] Amrit uses Black Dog as an example of how messaging can be used to send signals to millennials, a group that represents a disproportionate share of future growth, without alienating the older generation, who in the case of a whisky brand will continue to make up a large proportion of the market in this transitional period.

Diageo has defined Black Dog's purpose to help achievers unwind and relax. That philosophy uses the metaphor that even the fastest race car needs a pit stop where it refuels and then heads off again. The attitude has been captured in the tagline 'Let the world wait'. Says Amrit:

> It's open to interpretation. Millennials say 'look, I deserve my break. I'm entitled to my time so everyone else, including my parents, can wait until I'm ready for them!' The older achiever says 'I'm entitled because I've achieved but this time is also useful to me in other ways'. So each group can interpret it in a way that's consistent with their worldview and belief system. It's an attitude that allows for multiple interpretations.

Understanding the millennial mindset

India's consumers may be younger on average than in developed markets. But the people charged with communicating with them are often not. The average age of a marketing professional in India will be older than their western contemporary. While the country is young and the median age was 27.9 years in 2017 (Statista, 2017)[9], the hierarchical nature of Indian corporate life, promotions premised on time served, means that a decision maker is unlikely to be under 35. To become a sales or marketing director at 40 is still ambitious. So the people responsible for understanding and marketing to millennial consumers have likely grown up in a different era. Amrit is well versed in millennial thinking and Diageo has evidently invested heavily in understanding that cohort both globally and in the Indian context. Many of his contemporaries lack the same zeal and zest. Their mindsets, expectations, career paths, and horizons are very different from those of the people they seek to influence. Some exceptions exist.

Shantanu Raj is one. He's a highflying millennial marketing professional. His early career claim to fame is to have launched the quintessentially millennial product the Red Velvet Cornetto while at HUL. He's been appointed a Kellogg's marketing director at just 31 years. As such he'll be breaking the traditional taboo of younger bosses managing older colleagues with longer tenure. He is modern Indian aspiration in the flesh. Part of the mass migration from rural to urban India, he was born in small-town Rajasthan, his parents both middle-class government employees – father a banker, mother a teacher. Schooled in Hindi medium until 8th grade (13 years) his parents saw potential and moved to the state capital Jaipur to enrol him in an English medium school from which he subsequently passed the competitive entry exam to the prestigious Delhi Indian Institute of Technology. Living in college digs in Delhi he studied engineering and found his wings. A campus-hire to ITC, the tobacco and now hotel and personal care company, he was deployed to India's metro cities as a management trainee. Later with an MBA under his belt he moved to HUL, the nation's FMCG (fast-moving consumer goods) giant and renowned as a breeding ground for hotshot Indian marketers. During a six-year stint, assignments took him across more of the country planning campaigns for washing products and then snack food. When I met him he was on gardening leave having quit to join a lean start-up-style team looking at innovation at Kellogg's, and just back from a silent ten-day *Vipassana* meditation retreat. Perched on my sofa (not bought from Pepperfry but delivered with minutes to spare before our guests arrived for Christmas Day lunch a couple of years ago in a comedy sketch worthy of the Marx Brothers) he makes up for ten days of silence. He speaks quickly and knowledgably and exudes confidence.

The millennial mindset has become his area of professional practice. He has an eye for disruptive brands that have got to grips with that attitude, not merely an age-defined group, more a state of mind. The motivation of young Indians, he agrees, is to find autonomy and freedom within the strictures of a traditional society:

> To find a way to stand out while working within the system, to seek individualism without upsetting the crowd. They want to be taken seriously. They're respectful but subtly subversive at the same time. Being individual, standing out from the crowd has become cool, but it's not at the expense of society's approval. They want to contribute, not rebel.

He continues, 'The job of the brand is to find and solve that overarching problem: "Let me help you stand out from the crowd, without pushing the boundaries too far"'.

Many examples exist across categories. He cites a couple.

Manyavar is a men's ethnic clothing brand founded at the turn of the millennium in Kolkata. It's found the perfect point of balance, Shantanu tells me. 'The signal to millennials is that you can take ownership and reinvent tradition. You can establish yourself, stand out, and look your best while firmly fitting into society. It is brilliantly pitched'. As a sponsor of three Indian Premier League (IPL) teams it has high recognition among a mass audience. Manyavar's 2018 TV commercials featuring India's hottest celebrity couple – India's cricket captain Virat Kohli and actress Anushka Sharma – invoke the blend of tradition and modernity that the brand seeks to portray. Impeccably attired in traditional ethic wear they share a very new age set of wedding vows including his willingness to cook 15 days a month and not watch season finales without her. The reinterpretation of tradition is stylishly captured. Among its other accolades it was awarded most admired brand in the 2015 Indian Apparel Awards (Indian Apparel, 2015).[10]

Another case study is deodorant FOGG, a challenger brand that in seven years has taken by storm a category that was dominated by the incumbent, Shantanu's former employer Unilever's Axe (Lynx in the UK and a handful of other markets). Says Shantanu:

> It launched with a story of functionality – 'the deo with no gas' – and has been able to continue reinventing itself. Its latest campaign is quite subversive in a subtle way. There's a challenge to authority that says 'don't take us lightly, don't underestimate, take me seriously'. It uses humour to take down an older generation that's traditionally not taken this generation seriously.

The approach is counter to the tested and tired message that a spray of scent will have girls throwing themselves at you. Several FOGG campaigns have gently poked fun at traditional authority figures. Millennials have lapped it up. FOGG, owned by Vini Cosmetics, now claims to lead the category with a 20 per cent market share (Rediff Business, 2017).[11]

The ability to take charge, be respected, and build an independent identity are foundational pillars of the millennial mindset. Brands that can get that job done, as FOGG has, often grow very quickly in segments experiencing exponential growth.

In search of loyalty

The challenge for brands operating in dynamic markets where young, new consumers have little experience and no historical ties to brands, is to maintain their interest and keep them coming back. It's made more complex when the job to be done is not just to deliver scented protection or a sharp-looking outfit but also to provide validation and autonomy – because other products in unrelated spheres are competing on that ticket too.

Brand loyalty looks different in this context. Loyalty is primarily a developed-market construct without the same meaning in emerging markets. When consumers have had long exposure to a brand, and where population and income growth are incremental, flat, or in decline, encouraging or incentivising customers to keep coming back is a sound strategy for retaining market share. Developed markets are in that sense pretty stagnant. Habits and loyalty are established. Movement between brands is limited. There's little in terms of new segments in a mature market while in an emerging market new ones appear, expand, and morph at great speed. When the interactions are in their infancy and habits are yet to be formed, loyalty is much less relevant. Where brand loyalty does exist in emerging markets it may be driven by lack of alternatives, or alternatives that are sub-standard, or because switching is too troublesome. A new wave of disruptors is emerging to challenge market leaders that fail to act as leaders and capitalise on the shallowness of whatever loyalty they feel they can claim. The banking sector is one ripe for such disturbance. In many instances old school institutions rest on their laurels and get away with delivering products and services that aren't built for the modern era. Challenger brands are crafting millennial products that offer a fundamentally different user experience. In 2016 Singaporean bank DBS launched India's first mobile-only bank. DBS Digibank is a paperless, branchless, AI- and biometric-enabled banking service. A customer's Aadhaar card is used for authentication and the bank claims a new account can be set up in 90 seconds. With no minimum balance needed and the ability to set up an account from a coffee shop, it's perfectly tuned to the millennial mindset. It is erasing friction from a notoriously cumbersome activity. For older customers the multiplicity of their banking relationships across many areas of financial provision may well deter them from shifting. While millennials are putting in place their financial relationships they are less inclined to stay put. Focus on convenience, as DBS has chosen to do with the aid of new age technologies, allows it to achieve rapid penetration.

Economic liberalisation has created an explosion of choice. For consumers it takes time and rehearsal to learn how to operate within that changed scenario. In that sense Indian millennial consumers are in a 'practice era', learning the ropes by trial and error. Opinions are formed, confidence and knowledge are built, on the move. Sometimes a helping hand is welcome and may be a way of forging loyalty.

Telecoms titan Vodafone is a company that's found a new job to be done. A decade ago its challenge was to get customers connected in huge numbers. Now it's focused on hand holding customers as they navigate the, sometimes intimidating, digital revolution. As its India CEO Sunil Sood puts it: 'The job is to walk our customers through the change'.

Days before I interviewed him Vodafone had unveiled its new global positioning: 'The future is exciting. Ready?' Earlier we looked at what that means for Vodafone's internal stakeholders and how it is walking employees through the disruption of digital. From a consumer-facing perspective there's much to be gained from offering a helping hand when the customer has limited experience and a narrow frame of reference. Providing navigational assistance is a great relationship-building tactic in a dynamic and perhaps daunting landscape. Speaking to *Marketing Week* Serpil Timuray, Vodafone Group's chief commercial operations and strategy officer, explained the thinking behind the new tagline:

> We were conscious that technology is really changing at a very fast pace … We thought we could take a role in bridging these new technologies that may not look accessible for everyone and making them very daily, simple, and useful. So we identified a customer need to understand better how these technologies will be in their daily lives and the customer need for a brand to partner with them.[12]

As a global strategy it has much to recommend it. In India, where many digitally native consumers are leapfrogging traditional media and personal computers and experiencing the internet for the first time via mobile, the gap to be bridged is broad. It's a far cry from what Vodafone traditionally saw as the job to be done. In a decade it has transformed its customer experience and reengineered its processes and portfolio to suit a local, millennial-led clientele. Advertising has been innovative, much of it tied to the massive annual jamboree that is the IPL, and the brand has seen itself as the hero rather than falling back on celebrity endorsement. When famous faces have been used they've been offbeat, and recognised for their authenticity and stagecraft rather than mainstream movie muscle (Best Media Info, 2017).[13]

Setting up a business in India requires patience. A time-consuming, often logic-less, energy-sapping series of interactions have to be navigated. There's no map. The World Bank's Ease of Doing Business ranking for India in 2009, when we were establishing our business, was 122 out of 181 countries (*Doing Business*, 2009).[14] That year's report identified 13 procedures involved in business establishment. The idea that these could be completed in 30 days was a major underestimate. The basket of activities that the World Bank uses is designed to produce a set of comparative data. Many of the real world tasks implicitly related to running a business are ignored. The hassles of opening a bank account, or getting a mobile phone connection are excluded. Registering to pay tax is included in the basket. The convoluted and archaic process of being allowed to pay VAT in India provided an eye-opening lesson in the workings of petty corruption and the eagle-eyed enthusiasm of junior bureaucrats to extract 'speed money'. These unmeasured tasks are a drain on the entrepreneurs' time and energy and add significant hidden costs to doing business. Getting a mobile connection with Vodafone was painful. In 2009 it was a paper-based system requiring the provision of a host of documents and accompanied by an assumption of mistrust on the part of the retail staff. Holding the customer's hand, walking them through the journey, wasn't on anyone's list of key performance indicators (KPIs).

This is not surprising when you consider that the rate at which mobile phones were being acquired in India at that time was phenomenal. More than 100 million units were sold in 2009 (Rediff Business, 2010).[15] No other industry has experienced such rapid growth in India, ever. Mobile phone companies struggled to keep pace with demand. In developed markets at that time mobile phone companies were falling over themselves to differentiate their service, compete on customer experience, and instil brand loyalty as the market, which had grown rapidly in the previous decade, stabilised. In India the game was to keep heads above water as the deluge swirled around. The priority was to get the next 100 million would-be customers connected. The task at hand was to provide connectivity. Customer experience and loyalty played a very distant second fiddle to market penetration.

Much has changed in nine years. Some of the friction associated with business set-up and allied tasks has been eliminated.

Sunil explained what this new positioning means in terms a journey to transform Vodafone India into an agile, future fit, digital enterprise.

> Our new positioning is a bold punt at being future fit. 'The future is exciting'. Sure. But for many people that also comes with a level of trepidation and fear. 'What does that mean for my life? Am I ready?' So our job as a brand is to take our customer's hand and walk him or her through that journey at his or her pace because each person has a different speed of adoption. Our role is to help them understand the excitement and enable that journey for them.

'Digital enablement' is core to the Vodafone strategy in India. Much investment capital has been bet on India's digital revolution and the mass opportunity of mobile penetration. Since Vodafone also has a strong B2B play, it's also working to enable small businesses to make the most of new technology offering some third-party applications such as the Google Suite and other products that it's building internally.

This notion of taking the customer by the hand is a very different mindset to a one-size-fits-all, take-it-or-leave-it attitude, not much evolved from CP Thomas's patronising suggestion that if you don't like it you can send the phone back.

Indian consumers have been patronised and taken for granted for generations. A powerful aspect of the millennial mindset is the desire to be taken seriously, and engaged in a conversation rather than be talked at. Brands that find that shared tone of voice acquire respect and from that foundation stone may be able to build some degree of loyalty. But it's meaning may be different to what we take it to mean in the west. Reinvention and freshness are paramount. Newness trumps longevity.

Sporting franchises in India offer a thought-provoking lens on brand loyalty. The IPL was established a decade ago and has rewritten the rulebook of cricket. The Twenty20 format of the game now dominates and attracts big sponsorship and marketing spend. An IPL match is a great place to see India's millennials in their natural habitat. As a metaphor for the shift from tradition to modernity it's apt: arcane protocols and the stuffy etiquette of test matches have been given 'out' and dispatched to the dressing room replaced at the crease by a young upstart full of energy and hungry for action. An IPL match is a thrilling spectacle of frenzy and fireworks. The atmosphere is electric and margins of success or failure often appear wafer thin. (It's not clear how close matches really are as, for all its modern trappings, this form of cricket is not immune to the cancer of corruption.) Fans will cheer the team that's winning and switch allegiance during the match. The spectacle is more important than the team for many in the stadium. Loyalty is to a degree to the format not necessarily to the individual team. The same can be seen in the relationship Indian's have with the hugely popular English Premier League. In England and other traditional footballing nations, allegiance is a local, visceral experience often passed down from generation to generation. My 12-year-old son's Indian friends will support different clubs from one season to the next depending on performance, or when a favoured player has switched. Loyalties are fluid. Allegiance shifts. Much of the appeal is the Premier League brand. (My boy remains committed to the 'family firm' West Ham United and ploughs a lonely furrow as the only kid in claret and blue for miles around!).

In a country where incomes are rising and the number of people entering the 'consuming class' is growing at speed, the options to move up the value chain are significant. This adds complexity to the notion of loyalty if we take it to mean returning to make new purchases. The price a newly affluent millennial is prepared to pay for a pair of trainers one year is up from the price she paid the previous year. A low-cost and durable option may be discarded for a once aspirational, now-affordable, fashion brand the next season. And the 'upgrade' is an important measure of social status. Swapping brands is a marker of aspiration and sign of progress. In Vadodara, quiff-sporting Jay with his new motorcycle (and first-time credit) will be trading in the bike for a bigger model within 18 months since its job is to do much more than get him from A to B.

In the hospitality sector millennial hotelier Amruda Nair is seeking to match the needs of a young customer set that's turned its back on loyalty and is instead driven by convenience and a desire to find Snapchat-worthy experiences to fill its social media feeds. The job to be done is much more than providing board and lodging. In past generations hotel groups could rely on long-standing relationships that saw customers return year after year. Now the choice has expanded and the buying mentality shifted. And crucially she says the approach of millennials to travel has changed. More frequent, shorter stays have become the norm. Weekend breaks are rising in popularity. A flourishing domestic aviation business and mid-range hotels have made leisure travel accessible and affordable in ways it wasn't for previous generations. A survey of Asian millennials with overseas travel experience found that 77 per cent said they choose destinations where they can do new activities and experiences. 61 per cent said they want a custom experience and only 38 per cent preferred a group-led, package tour (*CNBC*, 2016).[16]

Amruda and her joint venture partner, Middle Eastern investor Al Faizal Holdings (*Business Standard*, 2016),[17] launched Aiana Hotels in 2016. 'We wanted to create something more accessible and experience oriented, designed to meet the needs of an emerging aspirational Indian traveller', she says. They're building an asset management model with a strong emphasis on its branded identity.

In the hospitality sector she says brands have lost control of the customer because they've ceded ground to aggregators and distributors. 'Booking.com is offering loyalty points!' she says with obvious frustration. So part of her agenda is to retake the initiative and build a brand that speaks directly to a young, well-travelled, and demanding clientele. That means accepting that the purchasing model has changed and customers want to pick and choose from a menu of add-ons rather than being dished up a one-size-fits-all package. The trend is another example of millennials' desire to take back control and to achieve autonomy. 'A good deal is important but convenience is more so. However they book, the challenge is to create an experience that can be customised easily on the go', she says.

Rickshaw owner Mahua Hazarika introduced me to another stand-out Indian brand that's servicing a growing demand among young consumers for experience and adventure while maintaining its traditional core constituency of older car buyers. Mahindra is a leading indigenous vehicle maker. It makes affordable, reliable, fuel-efficient cars and trucks across the country. Mahindra Adventure has found favour with young people who can't yet afford a performance vehicle but who've bought into the lifestyle and want the thrill of an off-road experience.

Says Mahua:

It's a kick-ass, experiential platform. The vehicles have a reputation for their rough and tough DNA. Mahindra Adventure lets you enrol with them and buy a range of experiences from a two-hour test drive to a 12-day Himalayan odyssey. It allows consumers to try out the vehicle, and be part of the club and pay for it. Essentially they've said 'pay me money to learn how to use my car'. It's been so successful agencies have stopped working on it because Mahindra now owns all the communications and they've created a platform that's home to all kinds of user-generated content. It gets the millennial mindset at just the right pitch.

Creating original content drives millennials' willingness to pay for experience. They may be less beholden to traditional markers of success but they're at the same time possibly the most status conscious group that's ever existed. The deal is not just the thrill of the ride but the opportunity to boast and brag about the event to their friends and 'frenemies' via Instagram and Facebook pages. Instagram naturally sees India as a vital piece of the puzzle as it strives to hit the billion-user milestone (*The Times of India*, 2017).[18] Mark Zuckerberg's creation had more than 240 million users in India in late 2017, making it the largest market for Facebook. Operating in 12 languages it has developed a localised offering that's made it a massive hit. But a market of such scale appeals to others too and in the aftermath of the company's data hacking controversy the chairman of Mahindra Group, Anand Mahindra, proposed to put his financial might behind an Indian competitor if one were to emerge. In neon-lit labs on the campus of IITs across India there are teams of engineers plotting cyber domination. Whereas in the past they would likely have been building a me-too product that localised an innovation built in a developed market, it's quite possible that the world's next multi-billion-dollar social/media platform will be conceived and built in India with the needs of its aspiring, optimistic young people at its heart.

Emerging-market consumers are younger and with different jobs to be done. They feel more optimistic about the future than do their wealthier, developed-market contemporaries (Deloitte, 2018).[19] This has a bearing on their response to brands and the relationships they are willing to build. There's less to fear in taking the plunge, occasionally getting it wrong, when the future looks bright. Switching brands is part of the 'practice era', a way of testing not just products but also themselves. A mass of new consumers with a positive outlook, eager to learn and willing to forge new relationships with brands that can find the right the balance at the tipping point of tradition and modernity.

I've identified a selection of brands that seem to have understood the millennial mindset. Some are millennial born while others have reinvented themselves to meet the rapidly changing demands of consumers who are being exposed to unprecedented choice and for whom newness trumps a long-standing relationship or so-called loyalty. They come from across many sectors but each offers lessons in how to succeed in the Indian context described earlier in the chapter.

IndiGo reaches the skies with an 'edgy' reinvention of the low-cost airline model

In 2008 travelling between Indian metros for a day of meetings was horrific. Buying airline tickets involved a travel agent. Domestic airports were dreadful. Facilities were rudimentary. The coffee was undrinkable. Taxi trips between the airport and offices had to be paid in cash. Delays were endemic. A decade on airline tickets can be booked online. Cabs are ordered either end via Uber or Ola. Cappuccino goes on a credit card. And there are

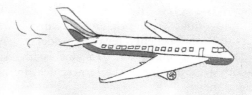

Figure 6.2

multiple airlines to choose from. Delhi fog still means that winter flights will be delayed but the whole experience exemplifies the meaningful changes that have occurred in the interim.

IndiGo, a low-cost airline founded a little over ten years ago, is a post-liberalisation success story. Since take-off in 2006, it has soared to become India's largest airline by fleet size and number of passengers carried. It had an impressive 39 per cent market share at the end of 2017 and almost 1,000 daily flights between 48 destinations. It is the fastest growing airline in the world's fastest growing aviation market (OAG, 2018).[20]

It's a characteristically millennial-minded product. Its brand essence is captured in the compelling, performance-centric and simple tagline 'on-time'. By contrast the national flag carrier Air India labours under the apt but uninspiring promise to be 'Truly Indian'. IndiGo's IATA designation '6E' has a playfulness that's carried through into the in-flight magazine and on-board food and beverage options. Fashion designer Rajesh Pratap Singh conceived the navy blue tunics accessorised with thin belts worn by female flight attendants who walk the aisles with Girl Power badges on their sleeves. Good quality service means it doesn't feel like a budget carrier. Judging by their attire and scant hand baggage, a good proportion of fellow passengers are business travellers.

Several of the millennials I interviewed listed IndiGo among the brands they felt appealed to the Indian millennial mindset. Hotelier Amruda Nair was one of the most voluble: 'I love it. It's Indian, but edgy. The advertising, the packaging, all have a sense of humour. Aesthetics appeal to me so I love the IndiGo blue. That's very Indian'. She tells me she chooses to fly IndiGo to Qatar, one of its seven international destinations, rather than the established Middle Eastern flag carriers.

IndiGo's success is built on much more than snappily dressed air stewards. It has reinvented the low-cost airline model. Before a ticket had been sold, or a baggage tag assigned, it struck a deal with airframe maker Airbus and ordered 100 A320s. By buying in volume it brought new aircraft into play at a low unit cost, bringing down maintenance costs and letting customers feel the benefits fewer less delays. As part of its ambitious growth strategy it inked a 2015 deal with Airbus for a further 250 narrow-body jets, making it the largest deal by number of aircraft for the European giant.

IndiGo's co-founder is Rahul Bhatia, the Canada-educated son of an Indian travel agent. Another Indian airline launched a few months earlier was the Vijay Mallya fronted Kingfisher Airlines. A drinks magnate he also read correctly the immense potential of India's aviation market. Kingfisher eschewed the low-cost model (*The Hindu*, 2017)[21] and fashioned itself on Virgin Airlines, the creation of another flamboyant showman. Kingfisher never turned a profit and by 2012 was mired in debt and ceased operations. It failed to understand the market and raised money on the then widely accepted assumption that a business could thrive on the presence of a high-profile businessman from an unrelated industry using a facsimile of a brand created in another part of the world. That sentiment still holds true among many 'promoter' families in India who believe that past achievement is a guarantor of future success. In the post-Independence era of the Licence Raj it may have been. In liberalised India, brand savvy, value-conscious customers take a different view.

IndiGo is one of the winners while Vijay Mallya is holed up in London as the Indian government seeks his extradition to face charges of money laundering and other crimes.

High in the mountains

You can pick marijuana leaves by the roadside in Manali. It's true. I've done so. But while processing and smoking the leaves is of course illegal, picking them carries no penalty.

Since adolescence the Himalayan hill station has held mythical appeal. For the mountains. Mostly. A habitual city-dweller I escape to the mountains to decompress. I'm an avid trekker and fell walker. It keeps me sane. Manali, a day's drive from the northern city of Chandigarh, is at an altitude of more than 2,000 metres above sea level. The air is thin. In the summer of 2017, under the artful leadership of Andre Morris, outdoorsman and founder of Outbound Adventure, I was part of a small group that trekked for nine days in the mountains that spur off from the Kullu Valley and the mighty Beas River. Our high point was the Chandrakhani Pass at 3,660 metres. The views from the snow line in May are spectacular. And not for the faint hearted. But first you have to spend a few days in Manali to acclimatise. There's not much to do except buy outdoor gear and smoke

Figure 6.3

hashish. The product from the neighbouring Parvati Valley is renowned for its potency. Because I spend some time each year in the English Lake District I'm fully stocked with mountain equipment: boots, gilets, jackets, socks, hats, backpacks, you name it, I've got second pairs and emergency options, and ones I was given for Christmas, and things in the sale that were too good to miss. So I didn't get waylaid with shopping.

Manali is something of a rite of passage for young Indians who flock there in the summer season. For the mountains, and the fresh air, and the white water rafting. I assume.

Newfound affluence means that the generation now headed up the Kullu Valley can afford to splash out on some decent and stylish protection from the elements. The French, alpine brand Quechua is ubiquitous. Evidence says it has taken a massive share of the market for outdoor and adventure apparel. Across the mountains, at every camp site and resting place, we came across entourages of student-age Indians decked out, many head-to-toe in Quechua products; boots, jackets, and hats; carrying Quechua backpacks and water bottles; sleeping in Quechua tents. It's a big change from a decade ago when I first trekked in India and you'd pass young people in makeshift apparel. Wearing sandals or plimsolls. In the snow.

Quechua has a global distribution deal with sports goods retailer Decathlon, which entered the Indian market in 2009 and now has stores in 60 cities, though not Manali, yet. Its warehouse outlets are stacked high with affordable clothing and other equipment. In late 2017 Decathlon inked a partnership with online retailer Flipkart, so even the armchair adventurer can be dressed for the mountains. Quechua seems to have got the magic equation of price, quality, and functionality just right and young people are flocking to the brand. Online reviews are overwhelmingly positive. Its dominance in the segment is astounding and suggests Quechua has not just read the mood of aspirational young Indians in search of new highs. It has largely created the market. As fitness and fashion continue to boom, other segments will become ripe for similar investments.

Paytm turns mass middle India on to mobile payments

Paytm is another of India's billion-dollar unicorns. Launched in 2010 it's risen meteorically to become the country's largest mobile payments and commerce platform. The name is an abbreviation for 'pay through mobile'. An emerging-market behemoth, Fast Company named it one of the world's 50 most innovative companies in early 2018.[22] Founder and Chairman Vijay Shekhar Sharma is youthful enough to be ranked by *Forbes* as India's youngest billionaire (*Business Today*, 2018).[23] Hagiographic newspaper stories present his as a rags-to-riches story. He's an outsider from Aligarh in the northern state of Uttar Pradesh, educated in Hindi medium and not an alumnus of one of the prestigious Indian Institutes of Technology or Indian Institutes of Management. There's an overwhelming preponderance of the latter in the start-up community in India – not surprising in a nation where networks and personal introductions are so important, but a situation that militates against whole communities of potential entrepreneurs and innovators who may have a more intuitive understanding of India's mass middle market or the bottom of the pyramid.

Figure 6.4

Paytm has produced a product that intuitively meets the needs of the aspirational young Indian consumer experiencing the rush of new and exciting spending options. In late 2017 Paytm had more than 250 million registered users, which suggests it has captured a huge share of the millennial wallet.

It was a winner in the unexpected and controversial demonetisation of 2016, when the government withdrew high denomination bank notes. Television showed queues of people stood in line outside banks in sweltering temperatures waiting to exchange their redundant rupees. News channels reported deaths. The government claimed it was a price worth paying to flush out so-called black money and drive digitisation. While the political and social debates raged, millions of people switched on to Paytm's mobile payment system, overnight (Exchange4Media, 2016).[24]

Ironically in March 2018 it may also be finding itself a victim of an allied Modi-led digitisation initiative, Aadhaar. The biometric identity system was meant to be a simplifier. The need to link an individual's Aadhaar to all service providers, including banks, payment wallets, and mobile phone companies, has added yet another layer of complexity and friction. The numbers abandoning will likely be small. But other headwinds exist. Messaging app WhatsApp (used by an estimated 230 million Indians and with much greater frequency [HT Media, 2018][25]) launched a payments service in February 2018. A Facebook-owned and therefore well-funded competitor may put a dent in Paytm's market dominance.

One of Paytm's great successes has been to place simple mobile-based banking services in the hands of many who were previously unbanked. It's part of an entrepreneurial ecosystem in which start-ups are finding opportunity to 'formalise the informal'. Cash payments are replaced by mobile transactions. Ola and Uber drivers become eligible for loans to buy cars. Small and medium enterprises in remote cities suddenly find they have access to vast new markets. The government hopes that many enterprises in the informal economy will be brought into the taxation regime. Motorcycle credit company CreditMate and gifting company Wedding Wish List are others mining the same formalising trend. CreditMate's founders received the seal of entrepreneurial approval by when Paytm took a stake in late 2017 (VC Circle, 2017).[26]

A deftness of touch when using social media is a common theme among the brands highlighted here. Paytm's ability to capitalise in the days after demonetisation, in a way that its competitors could not, has been attributed to its use of video-based social posts (XOR Labs, 2017).[27] Paytm has also been an active listener, using Facebook and Twitter to build its profile and reputation. In large part that seems to have been part of a strategy to build trust. The traditional and endemic trust deficit in India is a challenge to companies asking consumers to put money into an initially unproven technology. For digital natives it's provided a reliable and highly accessible payments method. They've taken to it in their droves.

Fast Company reported CEO Renu Satti saying that he aims for Paytm to reach 500 million users in the next two to three years.[28] A newly launched Paytm for business is a move up the value chain and part of that next phase of growth. Initially trialled in the southern state of Tamil Nadu the app is available in ten local languages, another indicator that Paytm has its finger on the pulse of mass market middle India.

Paper Boat repackages the tastes of childhood

Travelling back from Bangalore to Mumbai late one evening (on an IndiGo flight) I was delighted to find that Paper Boat drinks were available on board.

Paper Boat is a $100-million drinks business owned by Bangalore-head-quartered Hector Beverages that seems to have got the blend of tradition and modernity spot on. Launched in 2013 by two former Coca-Cola executives, the brand sells authentic, traditional Indian drinks in contemporary single-serve paper-coated packages. Flavours include such evocative and tangy fruits as jamun (*Syzygium cumini* or black plum) and kokum (*Garcinia indica*). 'It triggers nostalgia, because the flavours take you back to childhood. The packaging is great. It's quirky but authentic', says Amruda Nair who's a big fan. The brand has pursued some interesting 'nostalgia' tie-ins including with the publisher of Indian classic 'teen' magazines Amar Chitra Katha, another brand with a long-standing claim to 'authenticity'.

With funding from marquee private equity shop Sequoia Capital among others Paper Boat has invested in manufacturing facilities in Delhi in the

Figure 6.5

north and Mysore in southern India. In partnership with Japanese giant Nissin Foods it has built its supply chain into Tier 2 cities and rural markets.

Paper Boat's flavours have found favour in the UK, Malaysia, Dubai, and the US where large populations of non-resident Indians want to retain connections to their homeland. However, its price point may be deterring mass-market penetration according to *The Economic Times* which reported that while growth had doubled in 2016, sales growth had slowed to 12.5 per cent in 2017.

It offers a lesson for brand owners, and investors, who are awestruck by the immense opportunity of India but fail to get to grips with the very real impediments to accessing the mass middle market. Some brands create significant growth as they penetrate quickly the easy-to-access urban markets but struggle to gain a foothold in the Tier 2 and smaller cities that will be the driving force of much future growth.

Made like a gun, goes like a bullet: Royal Enfield nails the millennial market

The mountains of Austria may by alive with the sound of music, but India's roads reverberate to the roar of the Royal Enfield Bullet. The iconic motorcycle is a massive hit with young Indians. Sales of Royal Enfield in 2010 were a meagre 20,000 units. In 11 months to February 2018 it shifted more than 740,000 units (Car and Bike, 2018).[29] The world's oldest motorcycle brand seems to have found the perfect blend of tradition and modernity and its parent company has been richly rewarded with a share price that matches the brand's muscular image.

Figure 6.6

The motorcycle's origins are in British weapons manufacture – though its another brand that many Indians believe to be indigenous. It was originally made by the Redditch-based Enfield Cycle Company and exported to India. Its image is rooted in the rough and tough of Raj-era Indian army life. In earlier incarnations the motorcycle was a heavy machine that required a heavyset man to kick start it and manage its weight. Poor reliability meant he had to be adept at roadside repairs too.

Indian automaker Eicher Motors now owns the brand. Founded in 1948, a year after Indian Independence, the company is a prime example of a corporate 'Midnight's Child'. It has evolved over the past seven decades and is one of modern India's great success stories. Using 21st-century technology and manufacturing best practice it churns out Royal Enfield motorcycles at a state-of-the-art, robot-operated production line in Chennai, Tamil Nadu. Under Eicher's guardianship the modern avatar has been reengineered so that it's lighter and better suited to the relatively slighter frames of Indians. It is far less likely to break down, so owners don't need to be part-time mechanics to enjoy the experience of owning an iconic vehicle. Stringent emissions standards are met. The aura of authority and power that the military heritage bestows has not been lost. Anecdotal evidence suggests more women are now drawn to the brand (*The Economic Times*, 2013).[30]

But Royal Enfield's success is not just about image and engineering. It has understood the experiential nature of the millennial mindset too. The retail experience is slick and compelling. A regular flow of new models and customisations keep showrooms fresh. A formidable feeling of community exists among owners and Royal Enfield has built on that with a host of events, including Himalayan adventures and tours of Tibet, adding to the sense of belonging and shared purpose. Royal Enfield is more than a means of transport. For many it's a lifestyle.

Eicher Motors, now a company with revenues in excess of a GBP1 billion per annum, has seen its stock skyrocket by upwards of 60,000 per cent from Rs48.75 in January 2000 to more than Rs31,000 in November 2017.

There are a multitude of cheaper options available when it comes to two-wheeler mobility but Royal Enfield has tapped the mood of India's millennials willing to invest in brands that reflect and amplify their aspiration.

Zomato's food app delivers the goods

The 'dabbawalas' of Mumbai have for more than a century delivered lunch boxes to office workers in the city. *Harvard Business Review* was so impressed with the model that it cited them in a case study. 'The Dabbawala System: On-Time Delivery, Every Time' (*Harvard Business Review*, 2010)[31] highlights the simplicity of the operating model, flat corporate culture, and phenomenally low failure rates – the first two not traits naturally associated with Indian enterprise. Logistics giant FedEx is among

Figure 6.7

covetous corporations reported to have come to study the model. Corporate honchos and visiting dignitaries have paid their respects to the *topi*-capped crusaders. Rain or shine, more than 150,000 *tiffins* (lunchboxes) are dispatched full and returned empty to their owners' suburban homes every day at very low cost.

Home delivery too is a well-established part of Indian culture. In urban settings, the local *kirana* (grocery) store, the chemist, the fruit seller, and off licence will all send a delivery boy within minutes of taking your order.

New mobile-enabled technology is disrupting ordering and conveyance models. With an eye on the seemingly colossal opportunity in such a populous country, private equity and venture capital funds have been pouring money into the 'foodtech' sector. Five years ago almost everyone in my office would have brought his or her own home-cooked lunch with him or her. Single guys may have subscribed to a tiffin service. Now, every day multiple food deliveries are ordered via mobile apps. Packages arrive at the designated hour. No cash changes hands. The order is linked to a payment wallet or netbanking service.

Eating out and ordering in have become markers of millennials' lives. Symptoms of a modern lifestyle that's more spontaneous, less planned. And, crucially in a culture where dietary choices are complex and often tied to notions of caste and ritual purity, the ability to make food decisions outside the home gives young people another new freedom. A chance to assert their independence and take ownership of their life choices. It's another example of the mobile phone's ability to break down traditional power structures.

Zomato is an Indian foodie app that allows customers to search for, rate, and book restaurants online and place food delivery orders. Valued at more than US$1 billion it was one of nine Indian unicorns at the end of 2017 (MensXP, 2018).[32] It has raised more than US$250 million since it was launched in 2008. Sequoia India – a persistent punter on Indian e-commerce – has been a faithful supporter. Some of that money has been used to build technology and it has funded global expansion. Zomato is an Indian export success that has extended its reach and now operates in more than 10,000 cities in 24 countries. Zomato is now available in markets as diverse as New Zealand and the Philippines, United Arab Emirates, and the UK. Eating and dining habits in all vary according to local custom. Success requires the ability to localise the product and service offering.

Recent rounds of funding, including money from Ant Financial (the payments division of Alibaba), have been used to pursue an inorganic growth strategy. Zomato has been an active acquirer, adding third-party delivery partners in India and established players in international markets to its portfolio of assets. It is part of a new breed of Indian start-ups with access to capital from experienced investors.

Zomato's communications in India are bright and witty. They tap into an irreverent, meme-driven millennial mindset. On occasion they've pushed the boundaries of (traditional) taste. Immediacy, authenticity, and fluency with social media when the mark has been overstepped seem (so far) to have saved the firm from any major reputational damage.

Zomato's meteoric rise and outward-looking strategy suggest two lessons. By expanding into international markets it has shown that services designed in India need not be limited to the Indian context. Whereas in the past Indian innovation tended to be piecemeal and fell into the category of 'jugaad' (the unscalable hack) a new breed of innovators are developing solutions with much broader, potentially global, appeal. Historically Indian brands have largely struggled to reinvent themselves and adapt to the 'tastes' of international audiences. Zomato has achieved this.

Data for October 2017 to March 2018 suggest Zomato averages 35 million users per month and around 10 million are in India (Similar Web, 2018).[33] The focus on growth in international markets may suggest that the India opportunity is capped and that the reach doesn't stretch beyond the affluent, urban middle class. That may be equivalent to the population of a small European country but indicates that penetrating the middle and bottom of the pyramid – the Holy Grail for investors into India's digital economy – is a tough ask.

Digitising the wedding list

A big fat Indian wedding is a sight to behold. At one lavish reception in the paddocks of Mahalaxmi Racecourse in Mumbai I witnessed a stack of

Figure 6.8

plates beyond anything I'd seen even in a hotel kitchen. Several thousand guests were fed at live food stations over the course of an evening. No expense was spared for the marriage of a wealthy businessman's eldest daughter.

Most of the 10 million-plus weddings that take place in India every year aren't this extreme but matrimonial spending is a huge market. KPMG estimates annual spending on marriage-related services to be US$57 billion (GBP40 billion). Many families succumb to social pressures to push the boundaries of what they can afford. Much debt is accumulated through wedding expenditure in urban and rural communities. With more than 100 million unmarried Indians between the age of 18 and 35 and half the total population under 29 years it's a sector that will boom for years to come. Matrimony is one of the institutions being disrupted by a millennial mindset. Some young people are challenging traditional attitudes about how they choose, or have their partner chosen for them, and the type of wedding they have.

A new wave of digital entrepreneurs is using technology to streamline and improve the way weddings are organised. Part of the digitising agenda is to help families get better utility from their nuptial expenditure. It's another example of formalising the informal.

Kanika Subbiah spent 16 years in the US – following a well-trodden path of elite university, tech company, and consulting gig – before returning to her roots in south India. Her reasons for returning include a mix of family commitments, to ensure her children have an Indian education, and because of the business opportunities in a fast-growing and dynamic market where millennials are finding a voice and shaking up old orders.

Her office is a converted bungalow in Chennai's RA Puram district, a warren of narrow boutique-lined lanes and low-rise buildings. Her team are young. Sat at communal, long, polished wooden tables that could have been teleported from Apple's Orchard Road store, they're busy building an online wedding list service. It's a break with tradition and one that's challenging cultural norms.

Wedding gifting is a spectacularly wasteful activity, according to Kanika. 'Ninety per cent of the non-cash gifts given at weddings are not useful and they're either not used or recycled by being passed on to others. As a society we've become resigned to that fact', she says.

She set up WeddingWishList.com in 2016. Gifting is not new to her, she already has a more mature corporate gift business called Cherry Tin, established three years earlier.

When she launched the wedding list service she had to do a lot of explaining since the concept of a wedding list was anathema to most Indians.

> The idea that you 'ask' for gifts, that you articulate an assumption that gifts will be given, makes some people uncomfortable. It's breaking a taboo. But more and more couples see the value of making sure that money is not wasted.

Kanika has just finished her first wedding season and uptake has been strongest, as you would expect, among predominately urban millennials born post 1991 so now of marriageable age. South and western India have been the most receptive regions to date. She and her team feel this reflects a more 'progressive mindset' and willingness on part of grandparents, parents, and soon-to-be-couples to embrace a more contemporary approach. She estimates that 70 per cent have been love marriages and the remainder arranged. That's not representative of the sector as a whole. And the real benefits of less wasted expenditure would be felt more acutely in 'middle and bottom of the pyramid groups' where the cost of a wedding is a much greater proportion of income. A wedding is a chance to set up a couple with household goods, but those carry a price tag beyond the reach of individual donors in low income families. A list means people can club together and buy higher value goods. By tying up with matrimonial companies – the plethora of agencies that act as intermediaries of arranged marriages – and investing heavily in social media to build awareness, she's confident that the appeal will spread.

As with all change, resistance exists. But in the main it is not a generational gap, according to Kanika. 'Some communities use weddings as a way of transferring wealth through gold, cash, and other assets. For them there's much less appeal in the wedding list'.

She speaks to soon-to-be-married couples every day and sees other trends being enabled by pervasive technology. These include digital invites for guests outside the circle of extended family for whom an ornately printed card, hand delivered no less, is fundamental to the wedding ritual. She's launched an app that lets couples communicate with guests. Gone are the days of disposable cameras left on tables. Now photos can be taken on smartphones and uploaded for all guests to see while the ceremony takes place.

If the model gathers pace among a broader mass market it has the potential to turn wasteful though well-meaning spending into a much more meaningful experience for young couples.

Puma finds the sweet spot where the stadium meets the street

In Pune, Maharashtra, Pawan Jani is tapping into the fitness market with his health club offering. The city's desk jockeys are a niche market of several million. Running is growing in popularity in Indian metros. There's an early morning 5 km or 10 km race to take part in almost every weekend, including in the monsoon season. Pinkathon raises awareness of women's fitness, attracting lycra- and sari-clad runners alike. Tier 2 cities are getting in on the act. Mumbai and Delhi hold world-class marathons where elite runners from around the world are joined by tens of thousands of local amateurs. Mass-market India holds mass appeal for sports brands.

Fashion tastes are changing too and sports apparel is big business. Foreign brands hold huge cachet for young Indians for whom they offer easy access to 'affordable luxury'.

Figure 6.9

German sportswear company Puma has made impressive inroads since it entered the market in 2006. With 2016 revenues of more than GBP100 million it's risen to become the country's biggest sports apparel brand. And it expects India to be one of its top five markets by 2020, up from eighth in 2016 (ISPO, 2017).[34] Its strategy has been to build a profile in both mainstream and challenger sports segments and, at the same time, attach itself to a grittier street music scene.

It has forged associations and sponsorships with massive sporting franchises such as the IPL. Now a decade old the IPL has revolutionised cricket and made Twenty20 the dominant version of the sport, much to the chagrin of traditionalists. Puma's eight-year tie-up with Virat Kohli, Indian cricket captain and star of the Royal Challengers Bangalore IPL team, is reported to be worth a breathtaking Rs1 billion (GBP11 million). Usain Bolt, Asafa Powell, and Boris Becker have all made celebrity appearances for the brand. Robert Pirès and Thierry Henry, former stars of Arsenal Football Club, have visited. Pirès plays for Goa FC in the Indian Super League (ISL) – a football franchise that has immense potential given the rising interest among young Indians in soccer as an alternative to cricket. Walk along Manori beach to the north of Mumbai on a weekday evening and footballing boys outnumber cricketers by five to one. That cricket captain Kohli is also the face of the soccer league is a sign of the fluidity of the Indian market and the power of the sports star.

Puma has spent big and spread its bets on sports associations – traditional and emerging. At the same time it's tied its colours to more contemporary urban culture. Street dance, graffiti, and rap artists feature in the Suede Gully campaign ('gully' translates from Hindi as 'alley'). Filmed in four Indian locations in four languages, it's a hyper-localised take on global street culture – a pop video set on a local train and in the narrow alleys of urban India. Its DNA is equal measure MTV and Bollywood. The brand may be imported but its style references are properly 'desi' – a term used to describe authentic, unadulterated Indian culture.

Debosmita Majumder, head of marketing, Puma (India), speaking to *The Drum* (2017),[35] said:

> Our strategy is to identify our target group and find an authentic voice to communicate to them, and present to them the brand in the way that they associate and relate to it. We always strive to create exciting yet engaging experiences for our consumers, so they understand that Puma wants to invest in them.

Puma's global head honcho, Björn Gulden says its part of the company's strategy to connect with 'generation hustle'. The epithet captures the millennial mindset: style conscious, edgy, and immediate. With both its sporting tie-ups and its street credentials Puma seems to have found an authenticity that appeals to India's aspiring young. Whether their dreams are of footballing or cricketing glory, hip-hop or street art, many are chasing them in German-designed, Indian-made sneakers.

Puma has long understood that the job to be done is not just putting shoes on feet. Trainers and other sportswear accessories are part of a style revolution that puts young Indians on a par with their contemporaries in other parts of the world. By holding a mirror to them and speaking in a local language Puma makes a powerful pitch.

Key takeaways

1 **Understand that the job to be done isn't purely functional.** By using Jobs Theory as a frame of reference we see that one of the tasks for contemporary brands in India is to help millennials find their place in a world that is changing at speed. They express a growing desire for autonomy but still need to feel included. Belonging remains a powerful source of identity and stimulus to purchasing decisions.

   The market is highly dynamic. Old constructs are crumbling. New ideas and opportunities are appearing from all directions. Go beyond offering functional solutions. Find ways to address the deep-seated desire to carve out an individual character without breaking boundaries.

   Royal Enfield does much more than provide a mobility solution. There are many cheaper ways to get around but few that deliver as much in terms of psychosocial value. Royal Enfield has reengineered its product but its success is largely due to its ability to let customers feel part of a community, empowering them in a manner that's rooted in traditional Indian values of authority and status. Harley Davidsons are rare on India's roads because few hanker after the 'outsider' status the American brand projects.

2 **Rethink loyalty.** As a consumer market India is evolving at great speed. New competitors enter and build market share quickly. Competition in most categories is fierce. Consumer profiles and the purchasing prospects available to them are all up in the air. They are willing and able to trade up quickly. Loyalty is a construct better suited to more mature and stable markets. In the past two decades the number of cars available to Indian buyers has boomed. Families switch quickly: the Tata Indica of my cousins quickly gave way to Maruti Suzuki's WagonR to be superseded by the Swift, then the Honda City, which was replaced by the Hyundai Verna and then the Skoda Rapid. Now they're trading up into the crowded and fast growth SUV market. In the UK my father has spent 40 years replacing one Volvo with another. The market dynamics are fundamentally different. Respond accordingly.

3 **Newness holds great appeal.** Find alternative parameters to loyalty. Penetration and visibility are important. Focus on innovation and keep developing new products and services rather than relying on past glories and counting on the same people coming back. Invest in the customer

experience and keep it fresh. Be willing to reinvent and reposition. Make customer service a differentiator.

4 **Fill voids, hand hold, and enable the customer journey.** Because so many Indian millennials are new consumers, without established buying patterns or trusted relationships with brands, they need assistance to navigate through new and uncharted territory. Don't assume knowledge but be willing to offer advice and put a helping hand at the heart of the brand promise. Show what's possible and what can be achieved. Be an enabler of lifestyle and aspiration as Pepperfry has. Be a source of trustworthy information and provide ways to connect market participants. Both are prevalent 'institutional voids' in India and therefore there are market opportunities for those who can fill the gaps.

Vodafone is seeking to walk with the customer through the excitement and trepidation of the digital era. Zomato has built its business on the model of an 'honest broker' sharer of information. That perceived genuineness is highly valuable. CreditMate is opening up a new purchasing journey for many who are new to credit.

5 **Localise and customise.** Much as international brands hold a cachet and appeal, young Indians increasingly relate to brands that are rooted in their local reality. Puma has plugged itself into Indian cultural as well as sporting arenas. Red Label, a tea brand, tells authentic stories in a localised setting with characters that Indian millennials readily relate to. Vodafone has built highly localised brand touch points – through its advertising and fan engagement activity around the IPL – and has been rewarded by being perceived as a local player.

In 2017 the number of Facebook users in India surpassed the number in the US (Barrons, 2017).[36] That Facebook operates in 11 Indian languages (Facebook, 2012)[37] has helped its growth. The massive imbalance in favour of phones with an Android operating system versus Apple's iOS in India has been boosted by the former's personalisation options. Develop products and services that can be customised. Enable the carving out of identity.

6 **Find signals that resonate with millennials without alienating older generations.** The shift in spending patterns is in its infancy. Parental control and sanction still hold sway. Because this is a period of transition brands must strive for inclusion. FOGG's communications send an anti-authoritarian signal but without offending a group that may still exert some financial control. Levi's advertising in India seems to have found a space, which is reasonably edgy but appealing to wide sections of society. IndiGo's product offering taps the millennial mindset but its aircraft are half full of Baby Boomers and Gen X business travellers. Drinks brands are treading a fine line to catch the eye of the young while keeping the ear of older drinkers.

For brand managers and marketers the ability to get close to consumers and understand emerging trends is paramount because the cultural shifts are taking place rapidly but unevenly.

Listen carefully. Use Indians' comfort with ambiguity to your advantage. Craft messages so that they that can be interpreted constructively from multiple viewpoints.

7 **Appreciate the complexity of India and its niche markets.** There are many Indias. Its immense scale and complexity makes it at once a massive opportunity and a huge test. Its development is uneven. The transition from tradition to modernity is happening at differing paces. Some places have reached tipping points, others not. Some regions and communities are more open to new models than others.

In the same way that a single European strategy doesn't make much sense in a region with more than 30 nationalities, a one-size-fits-all plan for India won't hold up on the ground. Don't reduce India to a single mantra. It is many things, some of which are contradictory, all at the same time. Recognise its multi-layered potential. Niche markets in India can be huge. English speakers are a minority group accounting for around 10 per cent of the population (BBC, 2012).[38] Yet that number is approximately twice the population of the UK and growing steadily as aspirant families opt for English medium education.

Notes

1 ET Brand Equity, 2018. Pepperfry rolls out a slew of ad films to mark its six-year birthday celebration. Available at https://brandequity.economictimes.india times.com/news/advertising/pepperfry-rolls-out-a-slew-of-ad-films-to-mark-its-six-year-birthday-celebration/62376222. Accessed on 23/07/2018.

2 TechSci Research, 2014. India furniture market forecast and opportunities, 2019. Available at www.techsciresearch.com/report/india-furniture-market-fore cast-and-opportunities-2019/359.html. Accessed on 23/07/2018.

3 *Harvard Business Review*, 2016. The 'jobs to be done' theory of innovation. Available at https://hbr.org/ideacast/2016/12/the-jobs-to-be-done-theory-of-inno vation. Accessed on 23/07/2018.

4 IKEA, 2018. About IKEA. Available at http://ikea.in/ikea-india. Accessed on 23/ 07/2018.

5 McKinsey & Co., 2012. Winning the $30 trillion decathlon: going for gold in emerging markets. Available at www.mckinsey.com/business-functions/strategy-and-corporate-finance/our-insights/winning-the-30-trillion-decathlon-going-for-gold-in-emerging-markets. Accessed on 23/07/2018.

6 Khanna T, Palepu KG, and Bullock R, 2010. *Winning in Emerging Markets: A Road Map for Strategy and Execution*, Harvard Business School. Available at www.hbs.edu/faculty/Pages/item.aspx?num=37467. Accessed on 23/07/2018.

7   Scroll.in, 2017. Two brothers get five years in jail for drinking alcohol in Bihar. Available at https://scroll.in/latest/843431/two-brothers-get-five-years-in-jail-for-drinking-alcohol-in-bihar. Accessed on 23/07/2018.

8   *The Times of India*, 2013. Black dog is world's fastest growing scotch. Available at https://timesofindia.indiatimes.com/business/india-business/Black-Dog-is-worlds-fastest-growing-scotch/articleshow/25669983.cms. Accessed on 23/07/2018.

9   Statista, 2017. Countries with the highest median age in 2017 (in years). Available at https://www.statista.com/statistics/264727/median-age-of-the-population-in-selected-countries/. Accessed on 23/07/2018.

10 Indian Apparel, 2015. Manyavar receives 'most admired brand of the year' award. Available at www.indian-apparel.com/blog/manyavar-receives-most-admired-brand-of-the-year-award/. Accessed on 23/07/2018.

11 Rediff Business, 2017. The race of deos: why FOGG is winning. Available at www.rediff.com/money/report/why-fogg-is-winning-race-of-deos-ads/20170203.htm. Accessed on 23/07/2018.

12 *Marketing Week*, 2017. Vodafone revamps positioning as it moves on from 'power to you'. Available at www.marketingweek.com/2017/10/05/vodafone-reveals-new-brand-positioning-scraps-power/. Accessed on 23/07/2018.

13 Best Media Info, 2017. The pug and ZooZoo are valuable brand assets for Vodafone India. We don't provide over-exposure to either: Siddharth Banerjee. Available at http://bestmediainfo.com/2017/02/the-pug-and-zoozoo-are-valuable-brand-assets-for-vodafone-india-we-dont-provide-over-exposure-to-either-siddharth-banerjee/. Accessed on 23/07/2018.

14 *Doing Business*, 2009. Comparing regulation in 181 economies. Available at www.doingbusiness.org/~/media/WBG/DoingBusiness/Documents/Annual-Reports/English/DB09-FullReport.pdf. Accessed on 23/07/2018.

15 Rediff Business, 2010. 101.54 mn mobile phones sold in India in 2009. Available at www.rediff.com/money/report/tech-102-point-54-mn-mobile-phones-sold-in-india-in-2009/20100402.htm. Accessed on 23/07/2018.

16 CNBC, 2016. Turns out millennials want very different travel experiences. 8 September. Available at https://sg.finance.yahoo.com/news/turns-asias-millennials-want-very-052416702.html. Accessed on 28/09/2018.

17 *Business Standard*, 2016. Aiana hotels and resorts plans hotel chain in India. Available at www.business-standard.com/article/companies/aiana-hotels-resorts-plans-hotel-chain-in-india-116072200669_1.html. Accessed on 23/07/2018.

18 *The Times of India*, 2017. India key driver on Instagram's path to 1 billion users, co-founder Mike Krieger says. Available at https://timesofindia.indiatimes.com/people/india-key-driver-on-instagrams-path-to-1-billion-users-co-founder-mike-krieger-says/articleshow/61680457.cms. Accessed on 23/07/2018.

19 Deloitte, 2018. The Deloitte millennial survey 2018. Available at www2.deloitte.com/global/en/pages/about-deloitte/articles/millennialsurvey.html. Accessed on 23/07/2018.

20 OAG, 2018. Top 10 fastest growing airlines amongst the world's top 50. Available at www.oag.com/top-10-fastest-growing-airlines-among-the-worlds-top-50. Accessed on 23/07/2018.

21 *The Hindu*, 2017. Kingfisher Airlines crisis: timeline. Available at www.the hindu.com/business/Industry/kingfisher-airlines-crisis-timeline/article14380262. ece1. Accessed on 23/07/2018.

22 Fast Company, nd. Paytm. Available at www.fastcompany.com/company/paytm. Accessed on 28/09/2018.

23 *Business Today*, 2018. Paytm founder Vijay Shekhar Sharma youngest Indian billionaire with net worth of $1.7 billion. Available at www.businesstoday.in/current/corporate/paytm-founder-vijay-shekhar-sharma-youngest-indian-billio naire-with-net-worth-of-over-1-billion/story/272150.html. Accessed on 28/09/2018.

24 Exchange4Media, 2016. Paytm withdraws ad on demonetisation following social media backlash. Available at www.exchange4media.com/Advertising/Paytm-withdraws-ad-on-demonetisation-following-social-media-backlash_66691.html. Accessed on 23/07/2018.

25 HT Media, 2018. What WhatsApp's payments push means for Paytm. Available at www.livemint.com/Industry/CCMlSrrtKBPNNhEuyaLy4L/What-WhatsApps-payments-push-means-for-Paytm.html. Accessed on 23/07/2018.

26 VC Circle, 2017. Paytm invests in online lending startup CreditMate. Available at www.vccircle.com/paytm-invests-in-online-lending-startup-creditmate/. Accessed on 23/07/2018.

27 XOR Labs, 2017. How PayTM used social media to outperform its competitors during demonetization. Available at www.xorlabs.in/blog/paytm-during-demoneti zation-outperformed-competitors-using-social-media/. Accessed on 23/07/2018.

28 Fast Company, nd. Paytm. Available at www.fastcompany.com/company/paytm. Accessed on 28/09/2018.

29 *Car and Bike*, 2018. Two-wheeler sales February 2018: Royal Enfield sales grow by 25 per cent. Available at https://auto.ndtv.com/news/two-wheeler-sales-february-2018-royal-enfield-sales-grow-by-25-per-cent-1818899. Accessed on 23/07/2018.

30 *The Economic Times*, 2013. Women overcoming the gender stereotype by riding Bullet, Harley and Suzuki superbikes. Available at https://economictimes.india times.com/industry/auto/news/two-wheelers/motorcycles/women-overcoming-the-gender-stereotype-by-riding-bullet-harley-and-suzuki-superbikes/articleshow/27773198.cms. Accessed on 23/07/2018.

31 *Harvard Business Review*, 2010. The dabbawala system: on-time delivery, every time. Available at https://hbr.org/product/the-dabbawala-system-on-time-deliv ery-every-time/610059-PDF-ENG. Accessed on 23/07/2018.

32 MensXP, 2018. A brief look at the 10 unicorn companies of India as of 2017. Available at www.mensxp.com/work-life/success-stories/40246-a-brief-look-at-the-10-unicorn-companies-of-india-as-of-2017.html. Accessed on 23/07/2018.

33 Similar Web, 2018. Zomato June 2018 overview. Available at www.similarweb. com/website/zomato.com#overview. Accessed on 23/07/2018.

34 ISPO, 2017. CEO Björn Gulden: Indian market becomes one of the most important markets for Puma. Available at www.ispo.com/en/companies/id_79711798/sporting-goods-sector-puma-ceo-bjoern-gulden-relies-on-india. html. Accessed on 23/07/2018.

35 *The Drum*, 2017. How Puma entered India as a latecomer and still became a leading sportswear brand. Available at www.thedrum.com/news/2017/12/05/how-puma-entered-india-latecomer-and-still-became-leading-sportswear-brand. Accessed on 23/07/2018.

36 Barrons, 2017. India Facebook users surpass US: is it demonetization, Apple? Available at www.barrons.com/articles/india-facebook-users-surpass-u-s-is-it-apple-demonetization-1499982716. Accessed on 23/07/2018.

37 Facebook, 2012. Facebook translations. Available at www.facebook.com/FacebookIndia/posts/131854216934926. Accessed on 23/07/2018.

38 BBC, 2012. English or Hinglish – which will India choose? Available at www.bbc.com/news/magazine-20500312. Accessed on 23/07/2018.

7 New realities making it on screen

Figure 7.1

The big Bollywood hits of early 2018 were *Padmaavat*, a retelling of an ancient mythological 'poem' that ends with the ritual *jauhar* (self-immolation) of a Rajput queen and her kinsfolk, and *Pad Man*, a true story about a Tamil man who invented a low-cost sanitary towel. Other than the first five letters of their names, and Hindi dialogue, they have nothing in common. The first represents the tradition of mainstream, big budget, all-singing, all-dancing Hindi movies with strong religious undertones. Much controversy accompanied its ultimate, though long-delayed, release including a bounty on the head of its female lead Deepika Padukone. Meanwhile *Pad Man* belongs to a growing, contemporary vein of biopics that take offbeat, everyday stories and bring them to mass audiences. With an established mainstream star at the helm, it took an impressive US$10 million over its opening weekend. Leading man Akshay Kumar's previous hit was a movie called *Toilet: A Love Story*, a satirical tale of open defecation in rural India. The net effect of the country's recent development is that its population has more mobile phones than toilets.

'Bollywood', as the Hindi film industry is almost universally known to the dismay of many of its practitioners, pumps out almost four times as many movies each year than does Hollywood (*Forbes*, 2014).[1] South India has multiple industries producing movies in Tamil, Telugu, Malayalam, and other languages. Bengali cinema goes by the nickname Tollywood – its epicentre is the Kolkata suburb of Tollygunge. Each serves a mass audience with its regional appeal and across the Indian diaspora, so the numbers are huge. Bollywood movies sold an impressive 2.2 billion tickets in 2016, almost double Hollywood's 1.31 billion (*The Infographics Show*, 2017).[2] In financial terms Hollywood dwarfs Bollywood. The former grossed an estimated US$11.37 billion in 2016 with Bollywood posting around US$2.32 billion. In the US the finance industry is on the east coast and the movie business is out west, separated by a continent. In India they're a few miles apart. The money men and women are in south Mumbai and the filmmakers' upmarket ghetto is to the north, in the seaside suburbs of Juhu and Versova. The film industry is a big employer in Mumbai and alongside the studios and production houses a thriving advertising film business has taken root. Money and movies in close proximity make a heady mix. Young hopefuls flock from across the country, lured by the lights and the chance of fame, to work in suspect conditions for meagre pay – so not unlike the US film industry. High power distance, combined with the unregulated nature of the business, mean those young people, especially women, whether aspiring to be on screen or behind the camera, are highly vulnerable to exploitation. As the page proofs of the book were being reviewed India's #MeToo moment exploded and stories of sexual abuse in cinema, the media, and politics tumbled out.

Traditional mainstream Bollywood fare tends towards the melodramatic, its themes are often religious with a strong moral dimension. Racism, sexism and stereotyped, rather one-dimensional, characters pop up with worrying predictability. The humour is slapstick and plots are hackneyed. Irony is in short supply. Storylines can be genre-bending and trope-laden: perfectly choreographed song and dance routines erupt with no warning from car chases; romance, thriller, comedy co-exist in one movie; women's hair is always windswept, even indoors; characters miraculously appear as if teleported onto snow-capped Alpine mountains, in the same clothes they were wearing a minute ago as the village monsoon drenched them. 'Less is more' is an alien concept – like queuing and stopping at red lights.

Pad Man, Toilet, and *Pink*, a courtroom drama about a woman's right to say 'No', are among a slew of 'real-life' releases that explore more meaningful subject areas. They indicate that the output of Bollywood movies is changing, albeit slowly, to reflect the interests of a younger generation of moviegoers less enamoured of the unattainable faraway aspiration of the past. The 2018 Valentine's Day release *Love Per Square Foot*, a quirky Hindu-boy-falls-for-Catholic-girl comedy, rooted in middle-class desire for property ownership, captures the spirit of contemporary urban India. It appeals to a generation whose worldview has transformed with the arrival of services such as Netflix, launched in India in 2017, and Amazon Prime. A world of affordable content suddenly arrived in the Indian millennial's back yard and it means they can watch the same movies and TV shows, at the same time, as their peers elsewhere in the world. On-demand has changed the landscape of entertainment and driven changes in what's produced, and how it gets made. In the past decade or so a new breed of movies such as *Zindagi Na Milegi Dobara* (You Won't Get This Life Again), *3 Idiots*, a coming of age movie based on the bestselling novel by Chetan Bhagat, and *Rang de Basanti* (Paint Me with the Colours of Spring) have broken new ground. All mainstream hits, each deals with contemporary subject areas and together they're part of a wave of Indian cinema that's giving voice to a contemporary millennial worldview. *Devi* (Goddess) goes further. It's a 2017 short film, the story of a lesbian relationship between an upper middle-class Delhi girl and a household maid. Directed by Karishma Dube it's been well received at international film festivals and opens up a host of controversial plotlines that were in the past taboo but are now acceptable to an audience whose reference points are no longer just Indian. A rise in biopics, more women-centric films, a focus on plot and authenticity rather than the disjointed escapism of the old era, all characterise an industry in flux.

Niraj Pamwani is a successful movie producer who splits his time between family life in rural Goa and a weekday studio in Mumbai's western suburbs. His past glories include *Happy New Year*, a 2014 record-breaking, Dubai-set, heist movie starring Shah Rukh Khan, one of a trio of 'King Khans' who dominate Bollywood's superstar firmament. Niraj's most recent production credit is for *Daddy*, a political crime drama based on real events in the former mills district of midtown Mumbai. As the cotton industry declined in the 1980s violent conflicts erupted over prime real estate, now redeveloped into malls and glass-curtained head offices of banks, telecoms, and pharmaceutical companies. These two movies demonstrate what he sees as a shift in the past decade from formulaic hero-led masala movies to grittier, real-life stories that require both funders and audiences to be bolder.

Toto's is a 'garage bar' in Bandra. Laid back, tatty round the edges, loved by locals, it comes complete with a VW Beetle chassis hanging from the ceiling and barmen dressed in orange jumpsuits who look like they've escaped from either a Super Mario video game, or Guantanamo Bay. Over the screech of 1990s power ballads that are the staple soundtrack, Niraj tells me:

> Today's audiences are much more cultured. Their reference points are broader. Before the 1990s the movie house was the only place to see a film. There was no choice. Then TV opened up and we had a generation

bred on MTV and imported entertainment. Now they have access to unlimited content through multiple devices so people are willing to take more risks and as a result the stories have become much more diverse and interesting.

Global forces exert influence throughout the process, he says:

Content today is so international. We have Indian movies shot in the US or Europe with crews from the UK, visual effects and post-production done in Eastern Europe, more tickets sold in China than any other market, and a version available, for example, in Peru with subtitles in Quechua. The industry has transformed beyond recognition.

The day I interviewed him Niraj was hosting a production team from Rome passing through Mumbai en route to Goa to shoot a music video for an Italian teen pop duo. The creative collaborations benefit all parties with shared knowledge and new partnerships.

Indian cinema in that sense is no longer a domestic industry. As a result there's been an improvement in quality and a much broader canvas for storytelling. Movie-making equipment has evolved and it now costs less to make great-looking content. Indian production houses play a vital role in the global industry, providing visual effects support to Hollywood's biggest studios using technology that's standard across the world. A symbiotic relationship and access to international content through digital channels means Hollywood production values have become the global benchmark. Indian audiences have no reason to put up with substandard stagecraft. That theme is close to the heart of Shiraz Mukherjee, author of *Tiger in You* (2016)[3] and a 20-year veteran of the Indian film business who began his career as a production assistant, as he says, 'sweeping camel shit off the beach at Madh Island', a frequently used location an hour's drive north of Mumbai. In the film business, as in most other areas of life in India in the past quarter decade, liberalisation has led to immense competition. Audiences are becoming more sophisticated. Says Shiraz:

What you once could have got away with you no longer can. The modern viewer won't be fooled. Now they want to see authenticity. And it's opened up new subject matters. Suddenly you're exposed to new influences. You see someone else has done it and you think, 'Oh we can say it like that?' And that inspires filmmakers and gives them new confidence to push the boundaries.

Now in his forties Shiraz keeps in shape playing football and says he still feels like part of 'the India youth brigade'. We met on the set of a movie called *Raag Desh*. Released in late 2017 it's the story of the Red Fort Trials, the courts martial of the leaders of the Indian National Army (INA), an armed force committed to Indian independence that fought alongside the Japanese against Allied Forces in South Asia during the latter part of the Second World War. Commercial cinema it was not. Backed by government money but poorly marketed, it played at picture houses for a week, garnered a modicum of critical acclaim, and then fell into obscurity. Shiraz was a scriptwriter on the movie. I played the moustachioed Sir Claude Auchinleck, commander-in-chief of the British Army in India: a man who understood that Britain's departure would not be aided, nor its legacy enriched, by making martyrs of the INA leaders. On a film set a lot of time is spent sitting in dusty corridors waiting for things to happen, so I was grateful for Shiraz's easy company and intelligent banter.

Shiraz's bread and butter is TV advertising, his clients include some of the brands noted earlier for their millennial mindshare. He describes a trend driven by two powerful forces and triggered by the arrival of the internet. 'Because we're in a digital age, the economics of the advertising and communications business has changed. Now you can distribute via the net and get a much greater reach at hardly any cost'. That's changed the business model and freed up budget for content development as the previously huge expenses to distribute have been slashed. Budgets that in the past paid for a 30 second TV ad and the vast cost to air it can now be spent to create a two- or three-minute piece of content that can be shared online at very low cost. An ancillary benefit, the second force, is a rise in storytelling, because brands have more time to play with. So digital advertising is now less about the brand image, the logo, a celebrity endorsement, and the product, and more about what the brand stands for. Says Shiraz: 'People are now talking about the culture of the brand and asking "What are you supporting?" "What do you stand for?" These are the conversations that brands are having with millennials. That's a big break from the past'.

And he's adamant that young Indians want content, whether in advertising or feature films, that's truly Indian. Indian storytelling. 'You might love the *chow mein* and gorge on pizza, but when you get home you want *dal and rice*'. Dal (lentils) and rice dishes, the staples of Indian cuisine, vary greatly across the country, each refined to regional sensibilities. 'So', he continues,

> this generation has been influenced by what they've seen from the west, but they want to be presented with truly Indian stories. We have few modern-day heroes so we've begun to look back in to our past to look for protagonists. You can no longer just repackage something that originated elsewhere.

Communication styles in the past tended to be functional rather than engaging. Brands have spieled monologues and much of 'corporate communications' tends to be puff. Authenticity, meaning, and purpose weren't much in evidence. In an era of digital devices a patriarch with control of the remote no longer makes content choices. A new, hungry generation is at the controls and making their individual decisions. A point that both Niraj and Shiraz make, and one echoed by Kanchi Pandya, a millennial filmmaker directing Gujarati language films in Ahmedabad, is the way the industry has become more professional in recent years. Clannish it remains (and in some places corrupt) but more technically skilled, ambitious, and outward-looking people who see it as a career option, rather than a fall back, are bringing a new aesthetic, and much-needed discipline, to film making. Voices are becoming more diverse and better representative of a cacophonous nation brimming with optimism and receptive to new ideas. With access to relatively cheap, high-quality digital production technology they're less beholden to traditional narratives and increasingly confident.

Indigenous brands are now less likely to ape the west but rather to look within, to see themselves within a current Indian context – one where traditional values still have a place but where modern sensibilities, including gender roles, are tested. Red Label, the Brooke Bond tea brand – not an obvious place to find ground-breaking communications – has developed a voice that pushes boundaries and challenges stereotypes without causing offence. Under the tagline 'Taste of togetherness' it has broached the subject of live-in relationships, majority India's prevailing anti-Muslim sentiment, and put on air the domestic life and insurance needs of a 'call girl'. Fashion retailer Fab Alley went much further in 2015 when it used stand up comedian Radhika Vaz to promote its product. Performing naked on stage she confronts the fashion industry's hold on women's image in the online ad 'What the fuck should I wear?' It's a radical piece of brand communications by any standards, let alone in a nation with such a conservative dominant culture.

Puma, Cadbury, and Vodafone are international brands that have understood the need to represent local identities and found contemporary, grassroots styles to adapt their stories to an Indian millennial mindset. Local-language content is a vital part of that storytelling and the economics of the industry make its production and distribution more viable than ever. Learning English is an aspirational activity for urbanising and ambitious young Indians and a massive, largely unregulated industry is flourishing around it. But entertainment will continue to be enjoyed in vernacular languages. Urban millennial audiences naturally flick between local-language movies, the best of world cinema, and the latest episodes of *Suits* or *Game of Thrones*, and building identities for themselves that blend an eclectic mix of all. Feeding that appetite for content and enabling young people to tell the stories that resonate and reflect their confidence and aspiration is an exciting prospect.

Key takeaways

1 **Aspiration is within touching distance.** Desire is no longer a foreign land only to be dreamed of and held as an ideal. Young Indians now have access to international content, brands, and ideas – the real thing, not cheap copies. 'On-demand' means they see broadcast entertainment at

the same time as their colleagues in other parts of the world. Their benchmarks have been raised. They want output quality that's on a par with the west. Second best isn't good enough.

In the past, mimicking western styles, with an occasional topcoat of Indian-ness, did the job. Now it won't cut it. Create and distribute content that has meaning to them and their reality. Meet global production standards to hold the interest of a fickle, overloaded, but hungry audience.

2 **Authenticity is in demand.** Modern Indian filmmaking is becoming less about imagined heroes and mythical avatars and more about real-world champions with whom the viewership can relate. Disconnected and fatuous plotlines are giving way to more realistic storytelling 'The audience won't be fooled', as Shiraz says. That goes for advertising as well as for feature films. Old stereotypes are being challenged. Not all heroes are male. Women are breadwinners and lesbian love crosses caste lines.

Consumers of content want authenticity. Don't be shy of confronting India's gritty reality but remember that some otherwise liberal and forward-thinking millennials remain highly sensitive to 'unadulterated' images of India broadcast to the world. *Toilet: A Love Affair*'s subject matter indicates a growing willingness to speak truth to power and acknowledge the terrible injustices of life in modern India in a mainstream entertainment format.

Young Indians get the reality. In many cases they are motivated to pursue and create change. Show you're unafraid to shy away from big issues and endeavour to be part of the solution.

3 **Localisation is key.** India can't be seen as a homogenous market. Local tastes vary greatly. Audiences are accustomed to localised content both in terms of the language in which it's presented and the stories told. Digital technology and the internet have changed the business model and made translation and versioning viable. Use digital production technology to get the most from budgets and uncover stories closer to markets. Use digital distribution technology to better segment and target audiences. Give voice to a more diverse set of perspectives. Join the trend towards more pinpointed and location-specific communications.

Its sheer scale means niche audiences in India are massive as the rude health of local-language cinema and advertising indicate.

Notes

1 *Forbes*, 2014. Bollywood: India's film industry by the numbers [Infographic]. Available at www.forbes.com/sites/niallmccarthy/2014/09/03/bollywood-indias-film-industry-by-the-numbers-infographic/#243648812488. Accessed on 23/07/2018.
2 *The Infographics Show*, 2017. Hollywood vs Bollywood. Available at www.theinfographicsshow.com/home-1/hollywood-vs-bollywood. Accessed on 23/07/2018.
3 Mukherjee S, 2018. *Tiger in You*, Niyogi Books.

8   Conclusion

To get to grips with India – its seemingly overwhelming complications, its unique journey from tradition to modernity, its significance in the forthcoming Asian Century – requires the ability to put aside preconceived and perhaps well-proven models and look with fresh eyes. To do so is to see a unique opportunity, one in which optimism is not the disease that *Midnight Children*'s Saleem Sinai feels and sees, but a prevailing emotion which underscores the attitudes and outlook of young India. The optimism has to be qualified because the old order remains powerful but unreformed in some ways. But optimism is a dominant and energising force.

Confidence is abundant

In the process of reviewing my notes and listening again to the recordings of my interviews I'm taken by how articulate, outwardly confident, and lacking in cynicism are the young Indians I met. Across the age bands, from those just out of their teens to the ones now in their mid-thirties, whether in relatively low-paid jobs in two-wheeler towns or building business empires and launching new brands in the mega cities, they exude an infectious energy. A few have drunk the proverbial Kool-Aid and feel entitled seeing themselves as part of a 'gilded generation' destined by dint of birth to participate in one of the greatest economic growth stories of all time. But the majority express no entitlement. Many exhibit a formidable sense of purpose. They feel the potential and express a desire to contribute to the next phase of India's growth and its emergence as a major economic power. Some are even returning from overseas, contributing to a 'brain gain' as they see the opportunities in a fast-growing economy. Several express a healthy urge to stay and contribute to their country, not migrate and underwrite someone else's growth story. Filmmakers, farmers, and fitness trainers alike, there is much for them to be excited and optimistic about.

What they are experiencing now has clear echoes of the sudden blossoming of opportunity and new potential felt by post-war baby boomers in the United States and Europe as they achieved adulthood through the 1950s and 1960s. Jobs aplenty fuelled rising wages. Consumerism and home ownership flourished and generated a very real sense that this was a generation that would be better off than its parents. That promise held true for a couple of generations and the delta of change they participated in was transformative.

But currently in western economies, the UK as much as any other (*The Guardian*, 2018),[1] a generation of millennials finds itself dispossessed and fearful. The growth escalator that pledged increased prosperity from generation to generation has not just stalled. For many it's gone into reverse. Home ownership has become a distant dream. Wage growth has flat-lined. Many developed economies are now stagnant or at best delivering small but unsustainable growth driven by automation, quantitative easing, and another round of cost cutting. The prevailing mood in many advanced economies is now of austerity and scarcity. The future is uncertain and the waters choppy.

The millennial experience in developed countries is therefore very different to that which prevails in India, and to a large degree, other emerging markets. For this reason the notion of a global millennial mindset is flawed. To understand the Indian millennial mindset, and the huge potential it offers, it is necessary to recognise the complex context out of which it has surfaced.

The change is seismic

Seventy years after a traumatic and blood-stained birth, India is experiencing a period of profound transformation. The pace of change has spluttered and stalled and then picked up momentum in the last quarter-century. The past decade has seen momentous change as the economy boomed and millennials made their presence felt and came to prominence both pushing an agenda of modernisation and responding to a glimpse of aspiration. The choices available to them in the workplace or on the high street have ballooned. Job prospects have multiplied and improved for large sections of the population, even if the volume of new jobs has not yet achieved its potential. Wage inflation is strong and is driving a new wave of consumerism and demand for all manner of goods and services across every market segment. No area of the economy has been left untouched by the changes that were triggered by the opening up of the economy and the dismantling of the pillars of the Licence Raj.

Many aspects of life have transformed. Many changes are positive. Infrastructure has improved. On the day I concluded writing this, the government announced that it had achieved its goal of electrifying every village in the country. The achievement is not without its critics and in reality many homes still lack access to electricity (*Business Today*, 2018),[2] but progress is being made. The increased ease of doing business and the allied reform agenda that has taken root are enablers for a new generation of value creators. Some changes are less appealing. Lifestyle diseases have taken hold (Fit the Quint, 2017)[3] and threaten much of the rising life expectancy seen since Independence. The vast numbers of cars and the congestion on back roads in suburbs, ill designed for such volume of traffic, is an obvious daily example of rising affluence and part of the price of economic growth.

The benefits of this growth have been unequally distributed and some aspects of life remain stubbornly unchanged. Enthusiasm and optimism, while real and exhilarating, must be tempered with an acknowledgement of the lack of inclusive growth and terrible realities that prevail for some sections of Indian society. A woman's life is worth less than a man's on many levels. This can be seen in the country's skewed sex ratio, which in 2011 was 943 women per 1,000 men (Office of the Registrar General and Census Commissioner, India, 2018),[4] up marginally in a decade. Violence and discrimination remain a fact of life for many Indian women. One way to measure the success of India's millennial cohort will be to watch how it responds to this challenge and the degree to which it can overturn outdated but persistent social traditions to write a more inclusive next chapter in the country's narrative.

India now finds itself at a tipping point. In the next year or two millennials will make up the largest group of employees, the majority of wage earners, and the dominant group of consumers.

In this moment of transformation, many institutions are being shaken. Family structures are shifting, morphing, and becoming smaller. Parental authority is loosening and being replaced by other peer group influencers. Digital and mobile technologies are playing an important role in creating new networks that connect people who previously were outside each other's firmaments. Whereas for decades India tried to play catch up and replicate what happened elsewhere, it is increasingly an originator and exporter of innovation as Zomato and Paytm illustrate.

Workplaces are being disrupted as young people enter the workforce in huge numbers, bringing with them a new set of career expectations. They demand faster progress, more autonomy, and greater flexibility. With unprecedented options they're less conformist and have high hopes. Traditional markers of professional success, such as length of tenure and status, are giving way to new measures such as pay hikes undreamed of by past generations, autonomy, regular recognition, respect, and the ability to work more closely with leaders. A flood of young Indians are throwing off the shackles of 'old-thinking', while in some quarters an older generation hang on to old certainties. Some organisations are further ahead in their transformations, realising the need to accommodate new models that recognise performance measured by output not input if they want to tap the potential of millennial energy. Others remain trapped in systems and rigid models based on seniority and deference.

Economic advancement is a strong and important motivator for young Indians. But I also often heard a strong sense of purpose described – a desire to make things better, to co-create value, to build communities, to make a contribution. Instant gratification is not a universal expectation. The trends are most prevalent in urban areas but they quickly radiate out to smaller conurbations.

This new generation with money to spend is translating its aspirations into a fresh, fast wave of consumerism. They are new consumers, younger and without established relationships to brands. This presents great opportunity for companies with products and services that can capture the Indian millennial mindset and tailor offerings that meet its specific needs. Those go beyond, for example, the need for mobility or furnishings or deodorant and encompass a host of other psychosocial needs related to identify and the search for meaning in a world in flux. Midnight's Grandchildren are letting go of the bonds of tradition and embracing modernity. The transition has a very distinctive Indian flavour.

So there is much to be excited about in young Indians' confidence and optimism.

Yet at the same time we must recognise what an unnerving experience it is for the participants. So much is in turmoil. The changes are multidimensional. Long-established sureties are disappearing. So, however confident and optimistic young Indians appear, many lack the frames of reference or the proficiencies to manage the change.

Beacons to show the way, signposts that speak to the unique Indian millennial moment, are in short supply. Therein lies the opportunity.

Hybrid, localised solutions are needed

Change is exciting for some, daunting for many. The winners in this moment of opportunity will be the ideas, people, organisations, and brands that can harness the optimism and aspiration while recognising the challenges posed by change at such scale.

Midnight's Grandchildren may exhibit some of the same traits and behaviours as their international contemporaries and they will converge over time. But their current standpoint, cultural biases, and daily realities are different. Their desire for autonomy is strong as is the wish to embrace modernity. Both are often less powerful forces than the need to belong and to respect tradition. Fear of being outcast is palpable.

For all its long-standing and much-vaunted democratic tradition, India has been a very authoritarian country. Paradigms are changing but the backdrop is that power distance is high. Individualism is low. People may have a vote but it's often cast as part of a vote bank deployed to serve the interests of a group rather than an individual. Many are ill equipped to be empowered and take responsibility for their own destinies. Newly exposed to choices in the retail world they haven't chalked out relationships with brands. They have no precedents for managing those.

However much western ideas, including workplace structures and rituals, or imported brands, may be seen as aspirational, airlifting in models or products developed elsewhere rarely achieves much success.

In the workplace you can't expect to introduce a Netflix-style free-for-all policy when people have limited if any prior experience of autonomous decision making. Contemporary engagement models that were largely developed in response to the arrival of millennial ambition in developed markets, where the changes being wrought were more evolutionary in nature, will need to be reimagined. Such approaches have great value but need to be modified to recognise the different cultural context that exists in India. Implicating people in the success of an enterprise when they have limited agency in every other area of life, including their choice of marriage partner, will inevitably be a challenge. These are the contradictions that define the Indian millennial context. Organisations that win the battle for talent in this dynamic environment will be the ones that can create hybrid solutions. In Chennai human resources leader PK has customised the Hofstede Cultural Dimensions Theory to make it specific to Saint Gobain's business in India. It lets him identify gaps and create policies to achieve India-specific goals. Systems and practices that focus a bit more on 'I' and a bit less on 'we', that give agency to individuals, are one example of this workplace policy agenda. Steel and recruitment entrepreneur Nikunj Shah is providing more regular feedback to expectant young employees and shortening the horizon of their performance targets. And ad agency owner Mahua Hazarika is making employment periods time bound and managing her team members' development accordingly. HR boss Nanda and his colleagues at Tata Chemicals are assuming innocence rather than guilt and developing policies that enable rather than police. At Hardskills Shoba Purushothaman and Anthony Hayward are delivering training packages that do much more than simply impart skills. Their courses are addressing these gaps in self-awareness and helping individuals craft new workplace identities. Each recognises the hand holding and investment needed to make these changes a reality when the prevailing culture has historically had other priorities.

Young Indian consumers have previously not had the freedom to make decisions. Other people held the purse strings, deciding what would be spent and when according to traditional systems. The unprecedented choice now available to them is not easy to navigate. A strategy of hand holding and trust building can be a powerful differentiator. Providing information, filling voids, enabling various customer journeys are important tasks. By undertaking and doing these jobs successfully, brands can participate, as partners, in the new consumers' journey of exploration. The jobs to be done are much more than functional tasks.

There's much hype about a middle class of 300–400 million people. *The Economist* has made few friends in India with its sustained critique of that received wisdom. The reality is that mass middle India does present a huge opportunity but it is far from an homogenous group. An emerging powerhouse of new economic growth does exist in 'middleweight cities' with complicated names. These will be the drivers of growth in the coming decades. They are home to millions of motorbike-owning, sneaker-wearing

'Jays', hungry to participate in the next phase of growth. Brand owners, investors, and entrepreneurs must recognise that the wants and expectations of these new consumers may not conform to established definitions of middle class and may vary greatly from one part of the country to another or even within communities.

Thinking of India as a single market is a mistake as, Kanika Subbiah's Wedding Wish List shows. Some communities will jump at the idea of a digital solution that improves the utility of their gifting. Others will see it as a challenge to established channels of wealth distribution and have no interest. CreditMate is having success by lending in communities that have traditionally been overlooked or deemed high risk. Royal Enfield has created demand by providing a mobility solution that also addresses an important aspect of identity – and can charge a premium in doing so. Quechua has created a market for affordable, yet stylish, outdoor gear by pitching the right balance of price, quality, and functionality to a cohort of newly affluent trekkers. FOGG has taken the deodorant segment by storm by adopting a tone of voice that thumbs its nose at traditional authority without overstepping the mark.

The ability to understand these nuances should be integral to any strategy that seeks to engage young India. Armed with that understanding one can proceed to identify the places and spaces where opportunity exists.

India's so-called demographic dividend statistically promises much. Midnight's Grandchildren have good reason to be optimistic. Change offers opportunity, and change on this scale means the opportunity is magnified exponentially. Success requires a willingness to embrace the chaos, to see the world through their eyes, to create customised localised solutions to meet the unique needs of the world's largest cohort of millennials.

Notes

1 *The Guardian*, 2018. Millennials are struggling: is it the fault of the baby boomers? Available at www.theguardian.com/society/2018/apr/29/millennials-struggling-is-it-fault-of-baby-boomers-intergenerational-fairness. Accessed on 23/07/2018.

2 *Business Today*, 2018. All villages electrified, but not all houses: PM Modi's mission far from complete. Available at www.businesstoday.in/current/economy-politics/all-villages-have-electricity-but-not-all-houses-pm-modi-mission-far-from-complete/story/275930.html. Accessed on 23/07/2018.

3 Fit the Quint, 2017. We need to talk about India's lifestyle disease burden. Available at https://fit.thequint.com/health-news/lancet-study-india-lifestyle-dis ease-burden-2. Accessed on 23/07/2018.

4 Office of the Registrar General and Census Commissioner, India, 2018. Sex ratio. Available at http://censusindia.gov.in/Census_Data_2001/India_at_glance/fsex. aspx. Accessed on 23/07/2018.

Index

Bandra Kurla Complex (BKC) 60
Bandra Station 57
Bangalore 69–72, 75–6, 99; *see also*
  Bengaluru
bank notes 22; *see also* demonetisation
Bank of England 9
banks (banking) 12, 47, 54, 115,
  125, 129
Barrons 136
bars 63, 70, 72
BCG 48
Beatles, The 60
Becker, Boris 134
behaviours 77, 96, 97, 102
beliefs 33, 35, 111
belonging 40, 43–4, 50, 76–7,
  128, 135
Bengaluru 32, 69
Best Media Info 116
Bhagat, Chetan 143
Bharatiya Janata Party (BJP) 24
Bhatia, Rahul 122
Bhatt, Bimal 55, 56
Bhatt, Parth 61
Bhavnagar 61
Bhubaneswar 19, 55
bias 44, 64
Bihar 112
Bill, Jonathan 47, 54, 55
biodata 45
biometrics 22, 115, 125
biopics 62, 141, 143
Black Dog 112
Blunt, James 60
Bollywood 61, 134, 141–7
Bolt, Usain 134
Bombay Then: Mumbai Now 49
*Boom Country: The New Wave of Indian
  entrepreneurship* 10, 87
Bose, Subash Chandra (Netaji) 8
Brahmins 39
brain drain 10
brain gain 57–9
brand ambassadors 111
brands 11, 13, 20, 53, 60, 72, 75,
  106–10, 135–7; challenger 115;
  IndiGo 120–2; loyalty 114–20;
  millenial mindset 112–14; mountains
  122–4; movies 145, 146; new
  influences 110–12; Paper Boat 126–7;
  Paytm 124–6; Puma 133–5; Royal
  Enfield 127–8; tradition vs modernity
  35, 42, 45, 47–8; wedding lists 130–3;

workplace 86, 91, 100; Zomato
  128–30
Britain *see* United Kingdom (UK)
British Broadcasting Corporation (BBC)
  21, 137
British East India Company 8
Brunner Mond 90
budgets 145, 147
buildings 21–2, 49, 56, 98, 132
business, ease of doing 60
business models 53, 145
Business Process Outsourcing
  (BPO) 70
Business Standard 18
Business Today 124
businesses, domestic 23
Businessline.com 80
businessmen 67, 122

Cadbury 146
Café Coffee Day (CCD) 45, 56, 108
campaigns 23, 134
campaigns, governmental 114
campuses 70, 99
campuses, corporate 64
candidates 98, 100
Car and Bike 127
careers 12, 53, 59, 64, 76, 113; tradition
  vs modernity 38, 43, 48; workplace
  81–2, 89, 92–3, 95, 99–100
cars 20, 65; brands 111, 119, 125, 135
Carwale 111
caste system 10–11, 15, 67–8, 71; brands
  129; movies 147; tradition vs
  modernity 34–5, 38–43; workplace 81
celebrities 114, 116, 134, 141, 145
censuses 17, 21, 41, 44
Centre for Civil Society 11
*CEO, Chief Engagement Officer:
  Turning Hierarchy Upside Down to
  Driver Performance* 88
Chakravorti, Bhaskar 22
challenges 42, 83, 98
Chandigarh 122
Chandrakhani Pass 122
change, cultural 80, 81, 86
characters 142
charitable trusts 90
Chaudhuri, Raj 57
Chennai 32, 75, 128, 132
Cherry Tin 132
Chhatrapati Shivaji Maharaj Terminus
  49, 65